TEACHING ART CREATIVELY

Teaching Art Creatively is packed with ideas and inspiration to enrich teachers' knowledge and understanding of art and design in the primary classroom. It synthesises the philosophical and practical elements of teaching, encouraging a move away from traditional didactic approaches to contemporary classroom pedagogies to develop children's creative potential.

With an emphasis on recognising the value of children's art and how to support children's creative and artistic processes, key topics explored include

- improving your own creativity, competence and confidence
- helping children become independent artists
- starting points and imaginative contexts for art and design
- individual, group and whole class work
- art inside and outside the classroom
- how to develop visual literacy
- the value of working alongside artists
- the contribution of art and design to children's overall creative development

Teaching Art Creatively offers a new model of visual arts education in the primary years. Illustrated throughout with examples of exciting projects, children's work and case studies of good practice, it will be essential reading for every professional who wishes to embed creative approaches to teaching in their classroom.

Penny Hay is an artist, educator and researcher; Reader in Creative Teaching and Learning, Senior Lecturer in Arts Education and Research Fellow at the Centre for Cultural and Creative Industries, Bath Spa University; and Director of Research, House of Imagination. Penny's PhD, awarded in 2018, focused on children's learning identity as artists.

THE LEARNING TO TEACH IN THE PRIMARY SCHOOL SERIES

Series Editor: Teresa Cremin, The Open University, UK

Teaching is an art form. It demands not only knowledge and understanding of the core areas of learning but also the ability to teach these creatively and foster learner creativity in the process. *The Learning to Teach in the Primary School Series* draws upon recent research which indicates the rich potential of creative teaching and learning, and explores what it means to teach creatively in the primary phase. It also responds to the evolving nature of subject teaching in a wider and more imaginatively framed 21st-century primary curriculum.

Designed to complement the textbook *Learning to Teach in the Primary School*, the well-informed, lively texts in this series offer support for student and practising teachers who want to develop more creative approaches to teaching and learning. Uniquely, the books highlight the importance of the teachers' own creative engagement and share a wealth of research informed ideas to enrich pedagogy and practice.

Titles in the series:

Teaching Geography Creatively, 2nd Edition
Edited by Stephen Scoffham

Teaching Science Creatively, 2nd Edition
Dan Davies and Deb McGregor

Teaching Religious Education Creatively
Edited by Sally Elton-Chalcraft

Applying Cross-Curricular Approaches Creatively
The Connecting Curriculum
Jonathan Barnes

Teaching Languages Creatively
Edited by Philip Hood

Teaching Physical Education Creatively, 2nd Edition
Angela Pickard and Patricia Maude

Teaching Mathematics Creatively, 3rd Edition
Linda Pound and Trisha Lee

Teaching Art Creatively
Penny Hay

Teaching English Creatively, 3rd Edition
Teresa Cremin

For more information about this series, please visit: https://www.routledge.com/Learning-to-Teach-in-the-Primary-School-Series/book-series/LTPS

TEACHING ART CREATIVELY

Penny Hay

LONDON AND NEW YORK

Cover image: Lisa Dynan

First published 2023
by Routledge
4 Park Square, Milton Park, Abingdon, Oxon OX14 4RN

and by Routledge
605 Third Avenue, New York, NY 10158

Routledge is an imprint of the Taylor & Francis Group, an informa business.

© 2023 Penny Hay

The right of Penny Hay to be identified as author of this work has been asserted in accordance with sections 77 and 78 of the Copyright, Designs and Patents Act 1988.

All rights reserved. No part of this book may be reprinted or reproduced or utilised in any form or by any electronic, mechanical, or other means, now known or hereafter invented, including photocopying and recording, or in any information storage or retrieval system, without permission in writing from the publishers.

Trademark notice: Product or corporate names may be trademarks or registered trademarks, and are used only for identification and explanation without intent to infringe.

British Library Cataloguing-in-Publication Data
A catalogue record for this book is available from the British Library.

Library of Congress Cataloging-in-Publication Data
Names: Hay, Penny, 1961- author.
Title: Teaching art creatively / Dr Penny Hay.
Description: Abingdon, Oxon : Routledge, 2023. | Includes bibliographical references and index.
Identifiers: LCCN 2022013363 | ISBN 9781138913950 (hardback) | ISBN 9781138913967 (paperback) | ISBN 9781315691114 (ebook)
Subjects: LCSH: Art--Study and teaching.
Classification: LCC N350 .H39 2023 | DDC 700.71--dc23/eng/20220709
LC record available at https://lccn.loc.gov/2022013363

ISBN: 978-1-138-91395-0 (hbk)
ISBN: 978-1-138-91396-7 (pbk)
ISBN: 978-1-315-69111-4 (ebk)

DOI: 10.4324/9781315691114

Typeset in Times New Roman and Helvetica Neue
by SPi Technologies India Pvt Ltd (Straive)

To **all** primary educators who strive daily to provide a creative education for **all** children, especially in the arts.

CONTENTS

	List of figures	ix
	Series editor's foreword	xi
	Acknowledgements	xv
1	Teaching art (even more) creatively	1
2	Art processes and practices	17
3	Contemporary art and children's art	54
4	Case studies	64
5	The role of the adult	91
6	The learning environment for art	114
7	Planning art experiences in the primary curriculum	128
8	Evaluation and assessment in primary art	137
9	Conclusions	154
	Appendix	160
	Index	180

FIGURES

1.1	Reception class, drawing wall at Moorlands Infant School, Bath	2
1.2	Peacock, St Stephen's Primary School, Bath	4
1.3	Drawing at St Andrew's Primary School, Bath	4
1.4	Child painting, age 8, Bath Welcomes Refugees	5
1.5	100 languages of expression	9
1.6	Exploring pastels, Year 6, Newbridge Primary School, Bath	12
2.1	Drawing, Year 1	17
2.2	Yinka Shonibare, The British Library, 2014	20
2.3	Drawing, Year 6	21
2.4	Painting on canvas, Year 4	26
2.5	Reception, drawing the sound of the wind	27
2.6	Diwali, drawing in Pastel, year 5	29
2.7	Drawing machine, forest of imagination	30
2.8	Reception, playing with mark-making, shapes and patterns	31
2.9	Drawing using Pastels and ink wash, Year 1	33
2.10	Sketchbooks, Year 5, School Without Walls	37
2.11	Sketchbook assignment, Year 3	39
2.12	Painting, Year 1, Batheaston Primary School	40
2.13	Painting, Year 2, St Saviour's Infant School	41
2.14	Using powder paint	42
2.15	Observational painting, Year 2	45
2.16	Construction, Year 3	46
2.17	Working with Clay, Year 2, St Vigor and St John Primary School, Chilcompton	48
2.18	Printmaking, Year 3	51
2.19	Using collage, Year 4, School Without Walls	52
3.1	Children's expression in 100 languages, Freshford Primary School	56
3.2	The Artful Thinking Palette, Project Zero, Harvard University	57
3.3	Studio Habits of Mind, Project Zero, Harvard University	57
3.4	Exploring Yoyoi Kusama's Polka Dots Installation, Year 4	59
3.5	Children visiting the Black Swan Gallery, Frome	60

FIGURES

4.1	Ship, Jamie, Age 6, Victoria Art Gallery, Bath	67
4.2	Ship, marker pen, by Jamie, Age 6	67
4.3	Jamie's story, Age 6	68
4.4	Outdoor Museum, Freshford Primary School	70
4.5	Tommy's book, St Stephen's Primary School, Bath	71
4.6	Year 4, Batheaston Primary School	72
4.7	Djordje Ozbolt Exhibition, Holburne Museum	73
4.8	David Hockney study	74
4.9	Geneve, Age 10, St Michael's Junior School, Bath	77
4.10	Art Placards, St Andrew's Primary School, Bath at the School of Art and Design, Bath Spa University	78
4.11	Sir Ken Robinson responding to the children's artwork on the Media Wall, Bath Spa University	82
4.12	Designing the canvas, Year 4, Batheaston Primary School	83
4.13	Small Worlds, Year 2, St Andrew's Primary School, Bath	85
4.14	Sounds of House, Year 3 children at St Andrew's School, Bath	86
4.15	Perry Harris artwork for Forest of Imagination	87
4.16	Clare Day, Clay Forest	88
4.17	Jess Palmer, Urban Forest	88
4.18	Clare Day, Gift to the Forest	89
4.19	Helen Lawrence, Edible Forest	90
5.1	Adults as companions in children's learning	91
5.2	Adults using sketchbooks alongside children	93
5.3	Teachers and children documenting learning, St Saviours Infant School, Bath	96
5.4	Education Inspection Framework 2019	111
5.5	Children reflecting together through drawing, Batheaston Primary School	112
6.1	Window installation, creative space, Batheaston Primary School	117
6.2	Creativity Fair, Batheaston Primary School	118
6.3	Year 2 display at St Vigor and St John Primary School, Chilcompton	124
7.1	Children exploring Edwina Bridgeman's exhibition, Victoria Art Gallery, Bath	131
7.2	Children exploring paint and mixed media on canvas	133
7.3	A Planning Matrix to adapt for your school	133
8.1	Sketchbooks, Year 2	138
8.2	'Being an Artist' workshops, discussion on using sketchbooks, Reception to Year 6	141
8.3	Learning Habits, St Vigor and St John School, Chilcompton	145
9.1	Three ways special school, Bath	154
9.2	Kinder Garden, Bath	158

SERIES EDITOR'S FOREWORD

Teresa Cremin

Creativity in education concerns almost everyone. Parents, carers and teachers all seek to support young people in developing cognitively, socially and emotionally in order that they can cope in an increasingly uncertain world. Creativity is central to this. It is a crucial twenty-first century competency which we urgently need to foster both in schooling and more widely in our increasingly complex, globalised and digital societies. In the last two decades increased interest in creativity and creative pedagogies has been evident in the work of educators and researchers, and politicians and political systems too have become more aware of the potential of creativity (European Commission, 2009; Spencer, Lucas and Claxton 2012). Today creative approaches to learning are of international interest, and teachers want to expand their repertoires of practice and nurture young learners' creativity.

Recognising that creativity and creative thinking are key skills for 2030s learners, the Organisation for Economic Co-operation and Development (OECD, 2018) is introducing a test of young people's creative thinking in 2021 in their suite of assessments for 15-year olds. This Programme for International Student Assessment (PISA) is highly influential on governments' worldwide, so we can be sure new space and attention will be given to creativity in the years to come - in policy, practice and research.

Other potent factors are shaping the 'creative turn'. As I have argued previously, the relentless quest for higher standards and curriculum coverage has often obscured the personal and affective dimensions of teaching and learning (Cremin, 2015, pp. xi), but in the context of the Covid-19 crisis, educators are as concerned about children's mental health and social and emotional wellbeing, as they are about their learning loss and academic 'catch-up'. The challenge of balancing both will require considerable creativity and a professional mindset characterised by imagination and flexibility, not compliance and conformity. The curriculum needs re-shaping and new priorities are likely to emerge.

> Rebalancing the curriculum now to make creativity, critical thinking, decision-making, critical thinking, problem-solving, collaboration, resilience and adaptability as prominent as English, maths, science, dance, history and philosophy is what we need to do
>
> (Lucas, 2020)

SERIES EDITOR'S FOREWORD

The Curriculum for Excellence in Scotland and the new Welsh Curriculum recognise and celebrate the role of creativity, and whilst the English curriculum does not profile it as clearly, the Durham Commission (2019) has developed a vision for promoting creativity in education. This collaboration between Arts Council England and Durham University, examined the benefits of a creative education for young people from birth to 25, with reference to economic growth, skills and social mobility; community identity and social engagement; and personal fulfilment and wellbeing. To realize its rich vision will take time, but many schools across the UK already seek to develop innovative curricula that interest and engage all children, and many teachers find renewed energy and enthusiasm through deploying creative pedagogies. However, their capacity to do so effectively relies upon a shared understanding of the concept of creativity and demands that the myths and mantras which surround it are confronted. For far too long the misconceptions that creativity is connected only to the arts and confined to a few particularly gifted individuals have held sway. We must move on.

While debates resound about the difference between the 'Big C' creativity of genius and the 'little c' creativity of the everyday, most scholars argue it involves the capacity to generate, reason and critically evaluate novel ideas and/or imaginary scenarios. It encompasses thinking through and solving problems, making connections, inventing and reinventing and flexing one's imaginative muscles in all aspects of learning and life. Looking forwards, the OECD's (2018) definition of creative thinking may well prove important. The OECD view it as:

> The competence to engage productively in an iterative process involving the generation, evaluation and improvement of ideas, that can result in novel and effective solutions
>
> (OECD Directorate for Education and Skills, 2018:6)

To nurture such competence, the profession needs to not only recognise that knowledge and creativity are two sides of the same coin, not polar opposites but also needs to use creative pedagogies effectively. Recently Kerry Chappell and I undertook a systematic review of the international literature in this area (spanning 1990 to 2018) in order to understand the nature of creative pedagogies in the years of formal schooling. We created inclusion and exclusion criteria and analysed closely the 35 included peer-reviewed papers from 14 countries. Finally, we identified seven characteristics of creative pedagogies, namely: generating and exploring ideas; co-constructing and collaborating; encouraging autonomy and agency; problem-solving; playfulness; risk-taking; and teacher creativity (Cremin and Chappell, 2019). The characteristic most frequently evidenced was generating and exploring ideas. Perhaps this is not surprising as making and investigating ideas is often associated with an ethos of openness in which strong teacher-student relationships exist alongside a balance of freedom and structure. In one of the studies for instance, the researchers noted practitioners breaking conventions and enabling students to learn from their teachers' mistakes (Henriksen and Mishra, 2015). The second most frequent characteristic of creative pedagogies was co-constructing and collaborating. This may well challenge the profession to shift from what Vlad Glăveanu (2010) describes as the 'I-paradigm' to the 'We-paradigm' of creative collaboration. In many of the research studies we reviewed, collaborative activity and teacher-student relationships were seen to be central to the co-construction of creative pedagogies.

Teachers' creativity also emerged as a characteristic of creative pedagogical practice, with evidence of teachers pioneering their way forwards in lessons, investing time in discussion and sharing their pleasure in creative processes. Such professionals not only recognise, value and exercise their own creativity, but also seek to promote creativity in others (Cremin 2009; Cremin et al. 2009). Perhaps, in tune with Eisner (2003), these practitioners recognise that teaching is an art form and that teachers benefit from viewing themselves as versatile artists in the classroom, drawing on their personal passions and creativity as they research and develop their practice. In exploring possibility thinking, which Anna Craft (2000) argues is at the heart of creativity in education, a team of us observed an interplay between teachers and children -both were involved in thinking their ways forwards as they immersed themselves in playful contexts, posed questions, showed imagination and self-determination, took risks and were innovative (Craft et al. 2012; Burnard et al. 2006; Cremin et al. 2006). A new pedagogy of possibility beckons…

However, support is needed to help teachers seize such possibilities and this is exactly what this series of books offers. It accompanies and complements the fourth edition of the textbook *Learning to Teach in the Primary School* (Cremin and Burnett, 2018), and aims to support teachers in developing as creative practitioners. The books do not merely offer practical strategies for classroom use, (though these abound), but far more importantly they seek to widen teachers' knowledge and understanding of the principles underpinning a creative approach. Principles based on research. The nine texts in the series engage with key areas of the primary curriculum, mediating research evidence and making accessible and engaging the different theoretical perspectives and scholarly arguments available. In the process, the series seeks to demonstrate the practical relevance and value of research to the teaching profession.

If you aspire to develop further as a research-informed practitioner and creative educator, then you will find much of value here to support your professional learning journey and enrich not only your pedagogy and practice, but the children's creativity in the process.

ABOUT THE SERIES EDITOR

Teresa Cremin is a Professor of Education (Literacy) at the Open University (OU). An ex-primary school teacher, a local authority staff development co-ordinator, and then a lecturer in Higher Education, Teresa taught student teachers, led CPD and undertook research for 19 years at Canterbury Christ Church University before moving to the OU where she predominantly engages in research and consultancy. A Fellow of the English Association, the Royal Society of the Arts and the Academy of Social Sciences, Teresa has served as President of the UK Reading Association and the UK Literacy Association, and on the Boards of BookTrust and the Poetry Archive. Currently she sits on the DfE English Hubs Council as a reading expert, chairs the DfE English Hubs Council Reading for Pleasure sub-committee, and the Advisory Board of the Paul Hamlyn Foundation Teacher Development Fund. Teresa also co-edits the journal *Thinking Skills and Creativity*.

SERIES EDITOR'S FOREWORD

Teresa has written and edited 30 books, including the popular *Learning to Teach in the Primary School* (with Cathy Burnett, Ed, 4th edition, Routledge 2018) and recently *Reading for Pleasure in the Digital Age* (with Natalia Kucirkova, Sage, 2020). Previous examples include *Writer Identity and the Teaching and Learning of Writing; Storytelling in Early Childhood: Enriching Language, Literacy and Culture,* (Routledge, 2017, edited collections); *Teaching English Creatively* (2016); *Researching Literacy Lives* (2015); and *Building Communities of Engaged Readers* (2014). Teresa is passionate about developing readers for life and leads a professional user-community website based on her research into volitional reading https://researchrichpedagogies.org/research/reading-for-pleasure The site supports over 100 OU/UKLA Teachers' Reading Groups and 30 HEIs partnerships across the country in order to enable the development of children's (and teachers') reading for pleasure.

REFERENCES

Burnard, P., Craft, A. and Cremin, T. (2006) Possibility thinking. *International Journal of Early Years Education*, 14(3), 243–62.

Craft, A. (2000) *Creativity Across the Primary Curriculum: Framing and Developing Practice*. London: Routledge Falmer.

Craft, A. (2000) Childhood in a digital age: creative challenges for educational futures, London Review of Education, 10(2), 173–190.

Cremin, T. (2009) Creative teaching and creative teachers. In A. Wilson (Ed.) *Creativity in Primary Education*. Exeter: Learning Matters, pp. 36–46.

Cremin, T. (2015) *Teaching English Creatively*. London: Routledge.

Cremin, T., Barnes, J. and Scoffham, S. (2009) *Creative Teaching for Tomorrow: Fostering a Creative State of Mind*. Deal: Future Creative.

Cremin, T., Burnard, P. and Craft, A. (2006) Pedagogy and possibility thinking in the early years. *International Journal of Thinking Skills and Creativity*, 1(2), 108–19.

Cremin, T. and Burnett, C. (eds.) (2018) *Learning to Teach in the Primary School* (3rd ed.). London: Routledge.

Cremin, T. and Chappell, K. (2019) Creative pedagogies: a systematic review. *Research Papers in Education*, 1–33.

The Durham Commission on Creativity and Education (2019) https://www.dur.ac.uk/resources/creativitycommission/DurhamReport.pdf

Eisner, E. (2003) Artistry in education. *Scandinavian Journal of Educational Research*, 47(3), 373–84.

European Commission (2009) *Manifesto of the European Ambassadors for the European Year of Creativity and Innovation*.

Glăveanu, V. P. (2010) Paradigms in the study of creativity: introducing the perspective of cultural psychology. *New Ideas in Psychology*, 28, 79–93.

Henriksen, D. and Mishra, P. (2015) We teach who we are: creativity in the lives and practices of accomplished teachers. *Teachers College Record*, 117, (7), 1–46.

Lucas, B. (2020) Lessons from lockdown. https://bigeducation.org/lfl-content/this-crisis-shows-creativity-and-critical-thinking-is-more-vital-that-ever-before/ (Accessed 23rd August 2020)

OECD (2018) *The Future of Education and Skills: Education 2030*. International: OECD.

Spencer, E., Lucas, B. and Claxton, G. (2012) *Progression in Creativity: Developing New Forms of Assessment – Final Research Report*. Newcastle: CCE.

ACKNOWLEDGEMENTS

Special thanks to all the children, parents, artists and educators involved in this work.

TEACHING ART (EVEN MORE) CREATIVELY

Everyone is an artist

– Joseph Beuys (1972)

Every child, no matter what their background or circumstance, is entitled to a high-quality art education, to express their ideas, thoughts and feelings and create meaning. This chapter establishes the core ideas that will be addressed throughout the book within the context of current, national educational initiatives, exploring and challenging current orthodoxies in arts education.

Children need to be valued and respected as artists and as 'rich in potential and creative from the moment of birth' (Rinaldi 2006). However, the current educational climate is potentially damaging to children's creative development – an overemphasis on prescription, performance and products denies children's true potential to develop ideas in art. If we value children as competent and creative, this changes the way we teach art.

Learning in and through art, craft and design is now an entitlement for every child age 5 to 14 in the UK. Experience of art is a crucial element in a broad and balanced curriculum – its role should be central and its contribution is vital. The National Curriculum (2014) gives an overview of expectations:

- produce creative work, exploring their ideas and recording their experiences
- evaluate and analyse creative works using the language of art, craft and design
- use a range of materials creatively to design and make products
- teach children to develop their techniques, including their control and their use of materials, with creativity

Art, craft and design are interrelated but not necessarily interchangeable; they share a common process to achieve different ends – art is essentially concerned with communicating ideas in visual form and making imagery in response to human experience; craft especially draws on specific skills and knowledge in using processes and materials; design involves individuals in understanding why the made environment and

TEACHING ART (EVEN MORE) CREATIVELY

artefacts are the way they are and how the future may be shaped. This book focuses on art and teaching it creatively.

WHY MAKE ART?

to tell stories	to have fun
to observe	to develop skills
to imagine	to record events
to express feelings	to communicate information
to explore ideas	to analyse
to fantasise	to decorate
to experiment	to make connections
to be individual	to understand concepts
to personalise experiences	to compare experiences
to play with ideas	to investigate
to doodle	to research
to dream	to celebrate
to communicate ideas and beliefs	to think
to tell jokes	to reflect

Figure 1.1 Reception class, drawing wall at Moorlands Infant School, Bath

THE POWER OF ART

Art improves the quality of the human condition and enriches our personal experience, allowing us to make sense of the world and make meaning. Art gives us a sense of identity; it stretches our thinking and expresses our emotions. Art helps us become more creative and flexible and increases our visual and tactile awareness and understanding. Art provides a unique form of communication, helping children to understand the world in which we live. Art gives us an opportunity to express their ideas and feelings about their own personal, social and cultural worlds.

Direct engagement in practical art activity gives children the opportunity of developing their visual thinking and expression. Children observe and interpret images and visual forms using their imagination and feelings to develop their understanding of themselves and others. The experience of art is a constant exploration of children's experience. Art involves making images in 2D and objects in 3D; in primary schools, this includes drawing, painting, sculpture, printmaking, collage, textiles, mixed media and digital media. Central to art practice are curiosity, experimentation and inventiveness.

MOTIVATIONS FOR MAKING

The motivations for making art are as varied as human experience. Art involves making personal responses to experience, to express ideas and feelings, using and developing imagination and creativity. Children should be invited to explore a range of themes based on personal and collective experience, working individually or in collaboration with others, on a variety of scales in different contexts.

Art is made for different purposes. Sometimes children will be involved in observing, interpreting and recording their responses to direct or remembered experience or using their imagination and sense of fantasy; other activities will involve illustration, narrative or expressive work or have a focus on the formal elements of art, including line, colour, tone, pattern, texture, form, shape and space. The motivation for the work may be to solve a problem or to communicate an idea, to tell a story or express an emotion, to observe closely or to analyse.

Responding to and evaluating the work of artists, craftspeople and designers from a variety of times and cultures can help to inspire making. Copying, however, is not recommended as art is a unique process to each individual. Giving children the freedom to follow their fascinations is an important part of teaching art creatively. Once children have been given permission to be artists in their own right, their interests and motivations increase.

MATERIALS, SKILLS AND PROCESSES

Visual art processes involve a broad range of materials, skills and processes in order to realise ideas principally by making images and objects. Working with a variety of processes creates opportunities for a high level of personal involvement and choice. By developing confidence and competence in a range of media, children can select appropriately and develop their personal responses and ideas. Each medium has its own integrity and characteristics; children can explore the potential for using different materials, in combination, to make visual statements and develop a sensitivity to the visual and tactile elements of art and design. These can be appropriately matched to individual interests and fascinations.

TEACHING ART (EVEN MORE) CREATIVELY

Figure 1.2 Peacock, St Stephen's Primary School, Bath

Figure 1.3 Drawing at St Andrew's Primary School, Bath

THE IMPORTANCE OF DRAWING

All of the national curricula and guidelines in the UK rightfully stress the need to investigate, explore and record through drawing. Drawing plays a vital role in exploring ideas and manipulating information as a means of analysing and solving problems. In the early stages in the primary school, drawing and writing are closely linked as ways of interpreting, responding and communicating ideas about the world. There are many functions of drawing which have different emphases: to respond to and record direct, felt, remembered or imagined experiences; to investigate, analyse and understand; to plan; to express; to communicate; or to explore ideas or as an art form in its own right. Through the medium of the sketchbook, it can also be a way of mapping experience and gathering information on a personal level. Drawing is, in essence, visual thinking.

RESPONDING TO ARTISTS' WORK

Art and design activities can be taken to include making, looking at, thinking about, talking about, feeling about, knowing about and responding to art, craft and design. Looking at and responding to artists' work develop children's ability to engage with an artwork and relate to it in a personal way. Engaging in the description, analysis and interpretation of art also involves responding through spoken or written language and other art forms such as music, dance or drama. Giving context to any artwork is important to help children see why and how art is made, by whom and for what purpose. Art offers children a way of investigating and exploring the visual world we live in, developing visual literacy to explore the value and relevance in different contexts, times and cultures.

Figure 1.4 Child painting, age 8, Bath Welcomes Refugees

LEARNING IN AND THROUGH ART

There is intrinsic value in learning in and about art, yet art also enhances learning in other areas of the curriculum and in other art forms by promoting curiosity, imagination and creativity. It encourages children to develop creative and critical thinking and find creative solutions to problems. Skills such as observation, recording and analysis inform the whole curriculum. Art promotes transferable skills such as self-management, communication, empathy and flexibility. The arts provide ways of saying things that often cannot be said in other ways: arts activities enable children to understand that the imagination and its development are not marginal but central to the development of the individual and society.

INSIDE AND OUTSIDE SCHOOL

Art and design activities take place inside and outside school. The formal sector of education has a responsibility to teach art and design as a subject in the curriculum. The informal sector also has an impact on the attitudes of children to art and design – visiting galleries and museums can inform personal, social and cultural values. Bringing the outside world into the school, and vice versa, can help to bridge the gap between the professional world of art and that of school, working with artists and the wider community. Extra-curricular opportunities, based on collaborative links with the community, offer children a wider view of art in the world. There is a dynamic and reciprocal relationship between art, education and artists: art allows individuals and communities the opportunity to explore their experiences of the world, the 'here and now' as well as the past and future. Art can also provide intrinsic enjoyment and interest throughout children's lives.

Activity: Points for discussion with colleagues
- value of art education
- classroom organisation and management
- media and resources
- responding to children's interests
- using artists' work in the classroom
- working with artists and visiting galleries
- using sketchbooks

Teaching art creatively
- develops the ability to use materials and techniques imaginatively and experimentally to explore ideas and images
- develops curiosity and creative thinking
- increases motivation and engagement
- has a significant long-term impact on children's skills and confidence
- supports children as individual learners, helping them achieve by learning in ways that suit their personal learning styles
- contributes strongly to a distinctive school ethos
- sends a message to families that the arts are valuable in our lives

BECOMING A 'LIFELONG CREATIVE LEARNER'

Creativity is described as having four characteristics (National Committee for Creative and Cultural Education 1999):

- It always involves thinking or behaving **imaginatively**.
- The activity is **purposeful**; that is, it is directed to achieving an objective.
- The process must generate something **original**.
- The outcome must be of value in relation to the objective.

Creative and reflective learners are likely to be more self-aware and self-critical; honest about themselves and open to criticism and feedback; objective in weighing up evidence; open to and prepared to try different approaches; curious to discover other approaches, motivated to improve, and more able to carry this into their independent learning.

Qualities include

- questioning and challenging
- making connections and seeing relationships
- envisaging what might be
- playing with ideas and keeping options open
- representing ideas in a variety of ways
- evaluating the effects of ideas and actions

SO WHAT DO WE MEAN BY TEACHING CREATIVELY?

Teaching art creatively means valuing the inherent processes of art in the way that we teach, showing how the creative process is manifested daily in the classroom. If we show this process in our teaching, children are more likely to understand how this affords their own creativity in art. Here are some of the processes that a teacher might focus on:

- creating an inspiring space in which to learn creatively
- inviting personal enquiry, giving children the freedom to follow their own fascinations – giving children ownership and agency
- valuing curiosity and research as habits of mind
- modelling creative and critical thinking
- generating ideas through research, experimentation and playfulness
- investigating and making while using a range of materials and processes
- giving responsive feedback and opening up debate and dialogue
- drawing on a rich resource bank of images and artefacts

Since the introduction of the National Curriculum in England, central policy in education has restricted learning by focusing too much on prescribed knowledge and the assessment of this. In recent years, schooling has focused primarily on the transmission of knowledge and skills. There is a growing concern that this has been accompanied by a narrowing of the curriculum; as a result, many of our young people are launching into adult life without the flexible creative thinking required for negotiating a complex world.

We now need to provide opportunities for creative learning for young people and for professional development in creative learning for educators. Teachers are calling for 'permission to take risks', to finally take ownership of their own creative role, to be involved with research and learning themselves to enable young people to take charge of their own learning. As adults, teachers are 'companions' in research and learning, helping young people to ask good questions for exploration, providing feedback, reflection and support.

WE ARE ALL GUARDIANS OF CHILDREN'S CREATIVITY

The arts offer a powerful language of meaning making to explore and express ideas, thoughts and feelings. Article 31 of the UN Convention on the Rights of the Child states that *'every child has the right to participate freely in cultural life and the arts.'* Arts education should not be a luxury for a few. It is a pedagogical tool essential to facilitate creativity, adaptability, and social and personal transformation.

Children have an innate capacity to be curious

They are explorers and creative knowledge builders. Inspired by real art, our work invites children to be immersed in learning inside and outside the classroom, building bridges between theory and reality, schools and communities, young people and their futures.

Children have the right to express themselves in 100 languages

Their thoughts, feelings, theories and ideas – to find and follow their fascinations.

Our image of the child and the adult are vital: learning from Loris Malaguzzi in Reggio Emilia:

> One of our strengths has been to start out from a very clear, very open declaration of our ideas about the young child. It is a highly optimistic vision of the child: a child who possesses many resources at birth, and with an extraordinary potential which has never ceased to amaze us; a child with the independent means to build up its own thought processes, ideas, questions and attempts at answers; with a high level of ability in conversing with adults, the ability to observe things and to reconstruct them in their entirety. This is a gifted child, for whom we need a gifted teacher. She is a co-constructor of knowledge and values together with children; she is a cultured and curious person, which means an inveterate border crosser; and she is a researcher, with an enquiring and critical mind.
>
> (Moss 2004)

Reggio's 'pedagogy of listening' means listening to thought – the ideas and theories, questions and answers of children – treating thought seriously and with respect, to make meaning from what is said, without preconceived ideas of what is correct or appropriate.

Reggio is seen as a complex of workshops or laboratories where children and adults are constantly experimenting, inventing and welcoming the new and unknown through 100 languages of expression.

■ ■ ■ ■ **TEACHING ART (EVEN MORE) CREATIVELY**

■ **Figure 1.5** 100 languages of expression

HOUSE OF IMAGINATION (FORMERLY 5×5×5=CREATIVITY)

House of Imagination is researching and supporting children and young people's creativity through partnerships between educational settings, artists and cultural centres

■ to embed creative and cultural education in schools and centralise its place in learning and teaching
■ to develop creative reflective practice and influence systemic educational change

Inspired by the approach in Reggio Emilia, *House of Imagination* is an ongoing research project involving artists, educators, parents and the cultural community in supporting young children's creativity and imagination. Initiated in 2000, *House of Imagination* originally involved five early years settings, five artists and five cultural centres working in partnership. The research is based on a view of all children as creative, competent and full of potential. The adults see themselves as *'researching children as they research the world'*.

House of Imagination supports and deepens creative learning and teaching. Engaging in such research provides rich possibilities for working creatively with children and cultural communities – it addresses national issues about the creative arts in society. We are exploring exciting ways in which the creative and cultural community can be involved in meaningful learning with young children and their whole families. By changing the emphasis to learning **from** children, the adults become re-focused and re-energised researchers. The adults' own professional development through a creative learning community is empowering them in their practice and giving them confidence to share their new understandings with colleagues, parents and the wider community. The development of sustainable learning environments that support children's active and creative learning requires continuing professional development and research. A commitment to intellectual curiosity, reflection and dialogue is paramount. We need to invest in the creative talent of individuals and build an educational culture that can change lives.

5 × 5 × 5 = creativity involves multi-professional teams work in partnership to support children and young people in environments of enquiry, challenging orthodoxies and developing new ways of thinking. Children working as artists allows children to have opportunities for exploration, with emphasis on using innovative approaches that stimulate the imagination and encourage independent thought. Developing these innovative and transformational projects, *House of Imagination* has integrated a creative and reflective pedagogy with research at the heart of the process, building a new culture of schooling that has as much to do with the cultivation of dispositions as with the acquisition of skills.

Creative values: a set of values based on the competence and strength of the child. Children are seen as creative and powerful learners and as people in their own right rather than as people preparing for adulthood. Concepts of participation and democracy, reciprocity between children and adults, the significance of play, flow and deep engagement are central tenets of the research. Emphasis is placed on developing an environment of enquiry, and attention is given to multi-modal learning.

Creative relationships: attentive, respectful adults and children working collaboratively are at the heart of *5 × 5 × 5=creativity*. The quality of attention given to children is vital to develop 'a pedagogy of listening' (Rinaldi 2006). Really listening to children's ideas, observing children and documenting their learning are central to this pedagogical approach. The research recognises learning as construction of meaning, including 'sustained shared thinking' when an adult works with children to develop intellectual habits of mind (Siraj-Blatchford *et al.* 2002), as well as the importance of a creative and reflective approach that enables choice, agency and relevance.

Creative environments: both physical and emotional environments are important, paying attention to space, time, resources and attention and drawing in part on the notion of the environment as the third educator. This focuses on developing an enabling context in supporting playfulness, encouraging self-confidence and self-esteem. The *5 × 5 × 5 = creativity* project sees documentation as vital in a creative learning environment, where learning communities are fostered, and shared learning episodes are sustained over time. As companions in learning, (please keep this) adults offer children time and space to develop ideas.

Creative learning behaviours, dispositions and 'schemas': learning includes supporting creative thinking and learning dispositions, and attention is given to holistic learning, learner agency, persistence, openness, reflection and willingness to take risks (Craft 2002). Children's 'schemas' (universal patterns underpinning behaviour) and learning dispositions (habits of mind, such as engagement, curiosity, resourcefulness and perseverance) are observed and supported. Close observation, listening, documentation, interpretation, reflection and dialogue are central to understanding children's learning dispositions.

The following principles underpin *House of Imagination* research:

TEACHING ART (EVEN MORE) CREATIVELY

Respect and research

5×5×5 is focused on exploring children researching and representing the world together, with adults supporting them. Our main focus is adults' scaffolding of children's enquiries and hypotheses about the world through creative values, behaviours and environments. We have faith in the creative capacity and competence of everyone, children and adults.

Individuals together

The research is based on a view of all children as creative and competent; the adults see themselves as *'researching children as they research the world'*, learning alongside children. As adults it is our role to facilitate and support children's depth of learning: by respecting children and taking time to make observations and connections with the children's thinking, we can refine our own efforts in supporting their learning more effectively.

Democracy and participation

This initiative depends on the collaborative working at all levels: with children and colleagues (artists, educators and cultural professionals), with parents and the community, all aspects of 5×5×5 are documented and thus made transparent and accessible to all participants.

Listening and the consequences

Underpinning all the work is the 'pedagogy of listening' (Carla Rinaldi). Everyone's worth and their contributions are recognised; children's ideas are heard and supported. When children are listened to and offered a creative environment, they 'take off'; they experience a sense of ownership and satisfaction that is lasting.

Professional development

Professional development for all the participants is an integral part of the project. The work is child-led, presenting practitioners with opportunities to re-evaluate how children learn and how to present their understanding and development of the curriculum. It also supports enquiry into our own adult learning journeys and our evaluations of our own learning processes.

'The Hundred Languages of Children' (Loris Malaguzzi)

Our evidence is that children spontaneously and creatively connect all forms of thinking and expressive representation, demonstrating their use of the 'hundred languages of children'. We recognise the many potential ways in which we can share our feelings, imagination and ideas and how very limited and narrow much educational practice is. This sharpens our thinking and challenges us to open up for all children the chance to express themselves through many forms.

TEACHING ART (EVEN MORE) CREATIVELY

Figure 1.6 Exploring pastels, Year 6, Newbridge Primary School, Bath

Making learning visible

Findings show that careful observations and documentation of children's words will provide insight into their ideas and understandings. Documentation is a reflective process that makes flexible planning possible and modifies the teaching and learning relationship. It informs our way of being with children – how we 'see' them and respond and relate to them – and ensures that children or childhood is not 'anonymous'. It improves our professional knowledge of how children think, feel and learn.

The key principles of *House of Imagination* in summary are the following:

- believing in the creative competence of all children from birth
- valuing children's enquiries and theories, within a culture of listening
- valuing adults as creative enablers and co-researchers
- supporting reflective practice and constant evaluation
- observing and documenting children's learning
- supporting children to express themselves in 'a hundred languages' (Malaguzzi in Edwards *et al.* 1998)
- collaborating with parents and the community

House of Imagination is a studio for children and young people to work alongside creative professionals – time space attention, co-production. Artists and creative professionals engage in open-ended, critically reflective and collaborative forms of engagement that are central to and inspired by the nature of creative practice itself. The link between creative practice and pedagogy is vital in making the creative learning visible. We currently suffer from 'National Curriculum children'. We want to participate in 'the creation of a new culture of schooling that has as much to do with the cultivation of dispositions as with the acquisition of skills'.

■ ■ ■ ■ TEACHING ART (EVEN MORE) CREATIVELY

ART IS TRANSFORMATIVE

Art is a powerful medium through which we can understand ourselves and transform the world around us – it can inspire, facilitate and educate. The arts are life-enriching – building blocks for essential life skills such as resilience, confidence, self-expression and motivation and a powerful tool for positive social change. Learning through arts and culture can increase cognitive abilities and improve both engagement and attainment. The arts teach children that problems can have more than one solution, that questions can have more than one answer and that there are many ways to see and interpret the world in subtle and extraordinary ways.

THE ARTS ALLOW THE EXPRESSION OF CHILDREN'S IMAGINATION, IDEAS AND THOUGHTS

The arts help children learn to say what often cannot be said in words alone. Imagination, design, creation and experimentation invite intrinsic motivation. We need to manifest creativity and democracy daily and provide thoughtful spaces to explore our imagination. Imagination allows us to conceive of alternative possibilities and new ideas. Through being encouraged to pose questions and to identify problems and issues together, learners can debate and discuss their thinking; they are brought into the heart of the teaching and learning process as co-participants.

THE WORLD IS CHANGING RAPIDLY

We need to manifest creativity and democracy daily and provide thoughtful spaces to explore our imagination. In the UK, there is a tendency toward ever more stringent measurement of learning and ranking of achievement, to the instrumentalisation of art and the disappearance of education. The World Economic Forum (2016) recommended three key skills for future society: creativity, critical thinking and complex problem solving. The case for creative education is compelling. The UK's creative industries are thriving. The sector is the fastest-growing part of the UK's economy, and British creativity is globally coveted, but there is a real danger of our destroying something we are very good at.

CHILDREN ARE GROWING UP IN AN INCREASINGLY INTERCONNECTED AND COMPLEX WORLD

They need to grow in a creative environment which allows them to develop their own ideas. The cultivation of playful dispositions will enable them to be creative and collaborative contributors to the world's challenges – giving children the time, space and attention to be curious, to imagine new possibilities, to shape their identities and futures, to explore ideas and questions creatively and to value uncertainty. High standards and creativity do not need to be polarised. Every child has a right to the arts, creativity and culture, no matter what their background or circumstance.

House of Imagination also contributed to the pilot for Arts Council England's (2013) seven quality principles in relation to work with children and young people:

1   striving for excellence
2   being authentic
3   being exciting, inspiring and engaging
4   ensuring a positive, child-centred experience
5   actively involving children and young people
6   providing a sense of personal progression
7   developing a sense of ownership and belonging

(Arts Council England 2013)

Here is the InSEA (International Society for Education Through Art) Manifesto that draws on a lot of these principles:

- All learners, regardless of age, nationality or background, should have entitlement and access to visual art education.
- Education through art inspires knowledge, appreciation and creation of culture.
- Culture is a basic human right. Culture promotes social justice and participation in contemporary societies. A strong democracy is an inclusive society. And an inclusive society is a strong democracy.
- All learners are entitled to an art education that deeply connects them to their world and to their cultural history. It creates openings and horizons for them to new ways of seeing, thinking, doing and being.
- Educational programmes and curriculum models should prepare citizens with confident flexible intelligences and creative verbal and non-verbal communication skills.
- Visual art education opens possibilities and opportunities for learners to discover themselves and their creativity, values, ethics, societies and cultures.
- Visual art education develops an understanding of creative practice through knowledge, understanding and production of art in contexts.
- Visual art education develops the abilities to think critically and imaginatively; it fosters/aims at intercultural understanding and an empathic commitment to cultural diversity.
- Visual art education should be systematic and be provided over a number of years, as it is a developmental process. Learners should engage with 'making' alongside learning about art.
- Visual art education develops a range of literacies and aesthetic dispositions, with a major focus on visual literacy and aesthetic assessment.
- Visual literacy is an essential skill in today's world. It encourages appreciation and understanding of visual communication and the ability to critically analyse and make meaningful images.
- Art encourages the development of many transferable skills which enhance learning in other curriculum areas.
- Visual arts in schools help students to understand themselves, building confidence and self-esteem, and contribute significantly to their own well-being.

Participation by children and young people in arts activities improves academic attainment, literacy skills, cognitive abilities and transferable skills (Cultural Learning Alliance 2017). Intensive arts experience is associated with increased capability in risk-taking, paying attention, perseverance, ownership of learning, collaboration, leadership, aspiration, and higher-order thinking skills and with reduced drop-out rates. The arts enhance children's creativity and engagement, helping them to develop personal and social capacities and nurturing their higher-order thinking. As teachers, we need to develop a clear rationale for teaching art creatively in order to show both the intrinsic and extrinsic benefits.

10 lessons that the arts teach (Eisner 2002)

1. **The arts teach children to make good judgements about qualitative relationships.** Unlike much of the curriculum in which correct answers and rules prevail, in the arts, it is judgement rather than rules that prevail.
2. **The arts teach children that problems can have more than one solution** and that questions can have more than one answer.
3. **The arts celebrate multiple perspectives.** One of their large lessons is that there are many ways to see and interpret the world.
4. **The arts teach children that, in complex forms of problem solving, purposes are seldom fixed but change with circumstance and opportunity.** Learning in the arts requires the ability and a willingness to surrender to the unanticipated possibilities of the work as it unfolds.
5. **The arts make vivid the fact that neither words in their literal form nor numbers exhaust what we can know.** The limits of our language do not define the limits of our cognition.
6. **The arts teach students that small differences can have large effects.** The arts traffic in subtleties.
7. **The arts teach students to think through and within a material.** All art forms employ some means through which images become real.
8. **The arts help children learn to say what cannot be said.** When children are invited to disclose what a work of art helps them feel, they must reach into their poetic capacities to find the words that will do the job.
9. **The arts enable us to have experience we can have from no other source** and through such experience to discover the range and variety of what we are capable of feeling.
10. **The arts' position in the school curriculum symbolizes to the young what adults believe is important.**

SUMMARY

Every child, no matter what their background or circumstance, is entitled to a high-quality art education, to express their ideas, thoughts and feelings and create meaning. This chapter has established the core ideas that will be addressed throughout the book within the context of current, national educational initiatives, exploring and challenging current orthodoxies in arts education.

REFERENCES AND FURTHER READING

Arts Council England (2013) Quality Principles Working with Children and Young People.
Bancroft, S., Fawcett, M., and Hay, P. (2008) *Researching Children Researching the World*. Stoke-on-Trent, UK: Trentham Books.
Beuys, J. (1972) The Word. In L. Durini (Ed.) (1997) *The Felt Hat: Joseph Beuys: A Life Told*. Milan: Charta.
Craft, A. (2002) *Creativity and the Early Years: A Lifewide Foundation*. London: Continuum.
Craft, A., Chappell, K., Cremin, T., and Jeffrey, B. (2015) *Creativity, Education and Society: Writings of Anna Craft*. Stoke-on-Trent, UK: Trentham Books.
Cultural Learning Alliance (2017). https://www.culturallearningalliance.org.uk/2017/
Edwards, C., Gandini, L., and Forman, G. (1998) *The Hundred Languages of Children: The Reggio Emilia Approach—Advanced Reflections*. Greenwich, CT: Ablex Publishing.
Eisner, E. (2002) *The Arts and the Creation of Mind*. New Haven, CT and London: Yale University Press.
Moss, P. (2004) *The Town of Reggio Emilia and its Schools*. Refocus Journal 25.
National Committee for Creative and Cultural Education (1999) *All Our Futures: Creativity, Culture and Education*. Sudbury, UK: Department for Education and Employment.
Rinaldi, C. (2006) *In Dialogue with Reggio: Listening, Researching and Learning*. Oxford: Routledge.
Siraj-Blatchford, I., Sylva, K., Muttock, S., Gilden, R., and Bell, D. (2002) *Researching Effective Pedagogy in the Early Years. DfES Research Report 365*. London: HMSO.
The National Curriculum (2014) Department for Education, England.
World Economic Forum (2016) Key Skills for Future Society.

SUGGESTED WEBSITES

http://houseofimagination.org/
http://www.forestofimagination.org.uk/
http://www.schoolwithoutwalls.org.uk/

ART PROCESSES AND PRACTICES

Figure 2.1 Drawing, Year 1

The purpose of this chapter is to outline the processes and practices in art and design and how these support children's creative learning. Discussion will include the following:

- creative practice in art and design education
- developing visual literacy and 'ways of seeing'
- celebrating cultural diversity and inclusion
- using visual journals and the importance of drawing
- art processes and practices in the primary classroom

ART PROCESSES AND PRACTICES

In this chapter, we will show what it means to teach art creatively in primary schools involving children in learning that promotes exploration and experimentation; investigating and making with a range of materials and processes; developing individual lines of enquiry; evaluating and reviewing artwork; and collaboration and co-enquiry.

CREATIVE PRACTICE IN ART AND DESIGN

Art and design invite children to make meaning in the world. Observation of and conversation with children who are making art can also provide a window into their worlds. Teaching art creatively can then support children in making sense of their experiences through engagement and purposeful activity. The art and design subject reports published by the Office for Standards in Education, Children's Services and Skills (Ofsted) over recent years have summarised evidence of good practice in teaching and learning. Below is a short-hand summary, in no particular order:

- large and small scales
- observation and imagination
- exploration and demonstration
- progress in drawing
- feedback leading to deeper understanding
- subtle and skilled use of assessment
- artists inspiring children's work
- peer feedback
- spiritual, moral, social and cultural development
- themes embracing personal interests and experiences
- sharing best practice
- responsive planning
- 'adventurous' drawing
- exposure to original artwork
- exposure to contemporary artwork
- high-level thinking and making
- sketchbooks used to review and refine work
- making connections
- purposeful and independent activity
- improvising with limited materials
- curiosity and creative thinking
- use of local environment
- local community links
- engaging projects
- strengthening links to design and technology
- teachers' professional development
- gallery and museum visits
- promoting wider opportunities
- invitation and challenge
- displays and exhibitions
- contemporary crafts

This is useful as a checklist to reflect on with colleagues to identify successes and areas for development. The National Curriculum proposes that children should be taught

ART PROCESSES AND PRACTICES

> **Key Stage 1 (KS1)**
>
> ■ about the work of a range of **artists, craft makers and designers,** describing the differences and similarities between different practices and disciplines and making links to their own work
>
> **Key Stage 2 (KS2)**
>
> ■ about **great artists, architects and designers** in history

However, the notion of 'great' artists is in question here as there are more artists across the globe than just the popular (but sadly dead/white) French painters who tend to frequent the primary art classroom! The following sections address the richness and purpose of exploring, responding to and making art, craft and design.

DEVELOPING VISUAL LITERACY AND 'WAYS OF SEEING'

Children will develop their art and design skills more readily if they are placed in the context of the wider world of art and design. By looking at and responding to the work of artists, craftspeople and designers, children will be able to develop their understanding in order to inform their own art making. Children should be encouraged to use a wide range of art and design work from their own immediate surroundings and from different times and places. Direct experience is particularly valuable, whether this is visiting a gallery or museum or working with visiting artists, craftspeople and designers.

Visual literacy is an essential life skill; 'the viewer is an active and subjective being, as it is acknowledged that his or her background, experiences and interests all contribute to his or her interpretation of what is seen and understood' (Raney 1999). Technical visual literacy skills can be developed through talking about the visual world in terms of the elements of art: For example, *What different shapes are there? What different colours are there?* Holistic visual literacy skills can be developed by giving children opportunities to discuss possible meanings of art, craft and design: *Why do you think the artist made this work? What does it mean to you?*

It is essential to encourage children to have their own views and opinions about any work that they may feel strongly about and explain what they like or dislike. It is valuable to make the link between criticising and understanding art and design and making their own art and design. Children should be encouraged to take responsibility for their own work to make informed judgements about its qualities, to discuss their own work and those of their peers and to act purposefully upon those judgements.

ART PROCESSES AND PRACTICES

Figure 2.2 Yinka Shonibare, The British Library, 2014

CELEBRATING CULTURAL DIVERSITY AND INCLUSION

It is important for children to engage with artists and makers of all cultures, to build a rich and broad curriculum that celebrates difference and diversity. The Institute of International Visual Arts (Iniva) profiles artists responding to themes of identity and representation. Social media, particularly Instagram, is a key resource for sharing artists of colour as well as organisations and galleries that are dedicated to exhibiting the work of Black, Asian and ethnic minority artists. For example, the October Gallery in London exhibits work from international artists and produces resources for educators. Children from ethnically diverse communities need to see positive images of themselves in the artwork shared with them to ensure a culturally and visually rich curriculum. Art inspires an empathetic approach to culture and citizenship, promoting mutual tolerance and enabling young people to appreciate difference and diversity.

Cultural diversity is really at the heart of art, craft and design as a cultural activity. Inspiring learning in galleries and museums

- supports and extends students' education and has other social benefits
- enhances educational standards and excellence with the help of teachers
- develops young people's life skills and knowledge of visual culture to enable them to access education, training and employment in the cultural sector and creative industries and contribute to the economy of the country

(Engage 2014)

STRATEGIES FOR EXPLORING DIFFERENT ASPECTS OF WORKS OF ART

Each of the following sections aims to provide a structure to introduce the work of artists, craftspeople and designers in the classroom. These terms of reference may

■ ■ ■ ■ **ART PROCESSES AND PRACTICES**

provide useful ways of exploring different aspects of art, craft and design, to encourage plural readings and the possibility of different interpretations.

Making connections

Children should be encouraged to make connections between other art and artists in different times, cultures and contexts and to look at similarities and differences in their work. The emphasis here is on interrogating images and looking for clues and 'reading' images.

Personal experience and personal response

Bringing our own personal experience to a work of art and developing our own interests are essential in making a personal response. The personal, social and cultural understanding that an individual brings to a work of art is an important aspect of responding to and interpreting images – and an acknowledgement that we all see things in different ways.

■ **Figure 2.3** Drawing, Year 6

Ideas, meanings and subject matter

This involves exploring the content of the work and what it is telling us through its title or form, whether implied or explicit.

Media and process

The artwork has its own visual and tactile qualities of form, shape, space, colour, tone, line, pattern and texture. Children may choose to focus on the physical properties of an artwork, such as the materials and process of making.

21

ART PROCESSES AND PRACTICES

Context

Investigating why, when and where a work was made, and by whom, can reveal diverse meanings about an artwork. Researching the context of a piece of work can offer a broad range of meanings and interpretations.

Contemporary links

Art and design are concerned with issues that often relate to children's individual interests or popular culture (or both).

Historical and cultural links

Encouraging children to recognise traditions, styles and genres provides access into the social history and culture of the time.

Approaches and ways of working

Artists work in different ways, each having a preferred approach and providing a diverse range of definitions for what constitutes an artwork. Some artists use a sketchbook or workbook which demonstrates a particular way of working.

Children could use the questions to guide their independent research in a visual journal.

Questions to promote discussion

These include key questions, some of which are generic and can be asked of any artwork:

Is it art?
What is art?
Why is it art?
How do you know?
Is it good?
Who says?
What is this type of art/craft/design?
When was it made?
Why was it made?
Who made it?
Has the work been made by an individual or a group of people?
What does it tell you about the people/person who made it?
What is it made of?
What qualities does it have? Consider its shape, colour, form, and so on.
What meaning does it have? To you? To the artist?
What value does it have? To the artist? To the bank?
Do you like it? Why or why not? Would other people like it?
Does it work? Why or why not?
How does it make you feel?

ART PROCESSES AND PRACTICES

What is happening?
Have you seen something like this before?
What does it remind you of?
What does it make you think about?
How have time and place influenced the artist's work?
What is the style or tradition?
What is the purpose of the work?
What do you think the artist's intention was?
How has the work been influenced by other art?

DEVELOPING LANGUAGE

Art and design provide a rich stimulus and a variety of contexts for the development of language and literacy as well as informing learning across the curriculum. The nature of art and design involves action and reflection and is a non-linguistic process. However, developing a vocabulary to 'talk, think, feel and know' about art and design is fundamental to learning. It is not an 'insider' language, but a way of describing, discussing or communicating ideas about works of art. Children need the opportunity to use their developing vocabulary as a means of understanding their own work as well as the work of others.

The teacher's role in developing language relies on

- developing children's vocabulary to help them express their ideas, thoughts and feelings
- developing a range of practical strategies for 'talking about art' and ways of encouraging children to make critical responses and judgements
- addressing the formal elements of art, craft and design
- developing the technical vocabulary of materials, techniques and processes
- using sketchbooks to develop a dialogue to inform children's development
- knowing when and when not to intervene (the quality of intervention)

Children should be encouraged to take responsibility for their own work to make informed judgements about its qualities, to discuss their own work and those of their peers and to act purposefully upon those judgements. It is essential to encourage children to have their own views and opinions about any work that they may feel strongly about and explain what they like or dislike. It is valuable to make the link between criticising and understanding art and design and making their own art and design. Often, they will be able to use the same techniques and skills they have observed artists using.

Language we use in describing art can be categorised into

- **descriptive** language, responding to sensory experience
- **critical** language, making informed responses to the content and meaning of work
- **technical** language of material processes and techniques
- **visual** language yet using **all** the senses to respond to formal elements of art, such as colour, tone, line, shape, texture, pattern, form, space and movement

ART PROCESSES AND PRACTICES

Vocabulary

Identifying processes
painting, drawing, scratching, pressing, building and squeezing
Responding to qualities
angular, curved, strange, smooth, rough, hard, patterned and heavy
Naming and labelling
different colours, materials, objects, matching and comparing
Making analogies

It looks like a… It reminds me of…
Through the use of a critical vocabulary, children can describe and evaluate their own and others' work with increasing complexity in the following areas:

Materials	Why were choices made?
	Did they work?
Processes	How were the materials used?
	Why was the process chosen?
	How successful was it?
Formal qualities	How has line, tone, shape, form, colour, pattern or texture been used?
	Have they been used in combination?
Content/ meaning	What is the work about?
	How does it make you feel?

Activity

In what ways can work in art, craft and design help to develop speaking, listening, writing and reading skills?
How can children's understanding of art, craft and design be enhanced by developing these skills?

Inviting a creative and critical response – some areas you can focus on with children

General observations	Description
Objective response	Interpretation
Subject matter	Analysis
Expressive qualities	Evaluation
Content	Meaning and context
Form	Visual and tactile qualities
Process	Media and technique
Mood	Atmosphere and feeling
Physical appearance	Visual and tactile qualities
Construction	Materials and techniques
Function	Purpose/Use
Design	Fitness for purpose
Value	Worth and context

■ ■ ■ ■ **ART PROCESSES AND PRACTICES**

Activity: Developing language

How do you involve children in these processes?

Analysing	Interpreting
Annotating	Interrogating
Answering	Investigating
Arguing	Justifying
Commenting	Labelling
Commentating	Making analogies
Communicating	Making judgements
Considering	Naming
Criticising	Outlining
Describing	Presuming
Evaluating	Recording
Explaining	Reflecting
Exploring meaning	Remarking
Expressing	Replying
Guessing	Responding
Hypothesising	Reviewing
Identifying processes	Speculating
Imagining	Summarising
Informing	Surmising
Inspecting	Telling stories

Teaching art creatively involves children in learning that invites curiosity, exploration and experimentation. Central to this is supporting children to think creatively through making, using a range of materials and processes and developing their own individual lines of enquiry as well as inviting collaboration and co-enquiry. Purposeful dialogue in reviewing and evaluating their artwork builds an ethos of trust and respect in the classroom.

EXPLORATION AND EXPERIMENTATION

Inviting children to encounter new art resources without prescribing an activity allows time to explore them for themselves, opening up possibilities for children's self-initiated enquiry. Experimentation, risk taking and exploring the unknown are valuable creative processes. Anna Craft (2001) called this 'little c creativity' – that everyone has the capacity for possibility thinking.

THE FORMAL ELEMENTS OF ART AND DESIGN

Like written language, art and design have a basic vocabulary which consists of **visual** and **tactile elements:**

Colour   Form   Line   Pattern   Shape   Space   Texture   Tone

> **Colour:** warm, cold, light, dark, pale, deep, vibrant, dull, pastel, pure, bright, contrast, complementary, earth, hue, shade and tin

ART PROCESSES AND PRACTICES

Form: natural, made, cuboid, spherical, cylindrical, conical, structure, volume, mass, weight, rigid and organic

Line: straight, curved, jagged, smooth, hard, soft, light, dark, thick, thin, long, short, broken, flowing, contour and outline

Pattern: regular, irregular, repeat, tessellating, symmetrical, natural, geometric, rotation, grid, rhythm, decorative and border

Shape: large, small, natural, made, geometric, symmetrical, negative, solid, simple, complex, mechanical and organic

Space: open, enclosed, narrow, busy, large, small, confined, broad, high, wide and atmospheric

Texture: rough, smooth, hard, soft, matt, shiny, waxy, coarse, glossy, scratchy, silky, wet, dry and feathery

Tone: light, dark, tint, shade, black, white, grey, shadow, highlight, contrast, monotone, high key and low key

Each has its own expressive power and can be combined in both 2D and 3D work to describe objects and events in the real and imagined world. Comparison between the elements also reveals their differences. Children will always be using at least one of the formal elements in their work and will need to explore the variety of each. There are many other elements and concepts of art and design that could also be used as a focus for children's artwork (e.g., scale, distortion, illusion, rhythm, movement, harmony, and symmetry balance). Children need to have the opportunity to focus on one or more in each activity to ensure that their understanding is deepened. They will be building a critical vocabulary with which to analyse their own work and the work of others.

Figure 2.4 Painting on canvas, Year 4

■ ■ ■ ■ **ART PROCESSES AND PRACTICES**

INVESTIGATING AND MAKING USING A RANGE OF MATERIALS AND PROCESSES

Each medium has its own integrity and characteristics – different 'affordances' or capacities for representing a concept or idea. Different materials can be used to deepen children's understanding of a particular theme or concept (e.g., fine line pen and ink to draw feathers and charcoal to draw landscapes). Used in combination, children can explore the potential for using different materials to make visual statements and develop a sensitivity to the visual and tactile elements of art and design.

THE PRACTICES OF ART AND DESIGN

The practices and processes of art encompass many different forms of art, craft and design. Practices and processes include drawing, painting, craft, design, collage, textiles, sculpture, architecture, photography, digital art and mixed media.

Art and design offer the opportunity to work with a broad range of materials, skills and processes in order to realise ideas principally by making images and artefacts. The range of materials, the scale of the work and the different techniques and skills to be employed can be limited or open. This breadth allows access to all individuals at a level which is appropriate to their needs and aptitudes. Working with a variety of processes creates opportunities for a high level of personal involvement and choice. By developing confidence and competence in a range of media, students can select appropriately and develop their personal responses and ideas. These can be appropriately matched to individual interests and concerns. The essential areas of learning are in

Drawing   Painting   Printmaking   Sculpture   Collage   Textiles   Digital Media

■ **Figure 2.5** Reception, drawing the sound of the wind

ART PROCESSES AND PRACTICES

Drawing

Drawing appears to be one of the most fundamental human activities. In the sense of 'mark-making', it frequently pre-dates the emergence of speech in young children. Throughout history there is evidence of people drawing to help them explain the world in which they live. Children draw with pencil on paper or with sticks in the sand to give their thoughts visual form. In all drawing, a mark is used to 'stand for' something else. It may be something observed, or an idea, or an exploration of the potential of marks for their own sake. Drawing can be an extraordinarily economical and powerful means of communication because people have an in-built ability to attribute meanings to marks. Marks and lines can describe shape, form, texture, pattern and movement; they can tell a story, express feelings, communicate ideas and show a design.

It is well recognised that children's drawing ability follows a reasonably consistent pattern of development. Beginning with scribble for the sake of mark-making, it quickly grows into what has become known as the 'schema'. At this stage, children use a repertoire of shapes, circles, ovals and lines, to symbolise whatever they wish to depict. They make big and prominent what they believe to be important and do not obey the rules of Western European realistic perspective. Throughout the primary years, children will continue to depend on an elaboration of these early schema as one way of communicating their ideas and observations.

Children's drawings perform a number of functions and representational accuracy should not be the only aspect which is significant to either the teacher or the child. Children will become fluent in number of different ways of drawing to be able to choose the most appropriate one and know about and enjoy the variety of drawings by other people.

The functions of drawing

It is essential to identify the purpose of a drawing activity in order to choose appropriate subject matter for children to be involved in a meaningful way.

Why do we draw?

to observe and help us look at things more carefully
to explain or describe
to give information, to communicate ideas or thoughts
to capture or record information
to remember and record experiences
to plan or work out ideas
to illustrate language
to create, to express
to practise the skill, to refine and make it a more useful form of communication
to doodle, to fantasise
to decorate and pattern
to amuse or entertain
to tell stories

■ ■ ■ ■ **ART PROCESSES AND PRACTICES**

Figure 2.6 Diwali, drawing in Pastel, Year 5

Activity: Discuss with your colleagues the purposes of drawing

Drawing is … communication, expression, illustration, sensation, representation, abstraction, concept, metaphor, symbol, technique, definition, observation, rules, values, work, inspiration, invention, language, and function.

Try these activities:

Change your speed.
Write an exhaustive list of subjects and draw the last thing on the list.
List the qualities you would like a drawing to have.
Look at artists drawings.
Use someone else's idea.
What is the best drawing you have ever seen? Copy its style.
Draw a line, draw another on one side of the line, then draw another line on one side of that line keep going …
Represent two opposites (e.g., big/small and bold/timid).
Draw like a child.
Write a word then transform the word so that it is no longer readable.
Make a drawing using only straight lines.
Make a drawing using three sizes of circles repeated in sequence of size.
Think of your favourite joke and draw it.
Draw something you think would be a nice present.
Get someone else to finish your drawing.
Decorate, decorate.
Draw something that is in bad taste.
Draw something that is ugly.
Draw something beautifully.
Use a different body part.
Fill the page with marks then use a rubber.

ART PROCESSES AND PRACTICES

> Draw the way your closest friend would draw.
> Choose a subject: faced with more than one choice do all in the one drawing.
> Draw something, do something to it, do it again.
> How many different marks, lines, tones, patterns, textures can you make?
> Collect visual information about a particular object or place.
> Make colour notes or 'swatches', take rubbings, draw fragments.
> Make a collection of cuttings and photographs around a theme; turn them into drawings
> Using a viewfinder, make a series of observational studies of natural and made objects; abstract them.
> Experiment with different media and mixed media.
> Make personal reflections on the meaning of your work.
> Find connections between the themes and ideas that you are recording, make annotations, write a series of questions …

Drawing materials and mark-making

It is important to encourage children to use a wide range of drawing tools and media to explore the range of possible marks, to articulate the properties and qualities of the marks and how they are made. Care should be taken that these materials are introduced to children gradually and that they are given the opportunity and time to get to know them and use them purposefully.

	biro/felt tips	*soft pastel/conte crayon soft pencils 2B/4B/6B chalk/charcoal*	*wax crayon oil pastel*	*ink*
properties	hard/linear	soft/smudgy	waxy/oily	wet/runny
processes	pressing	smudging	scratching	overlaying
variables	pressure	surface	rhythm	direction
qualities	dark	smooth	textured	translucent

Figure 2.7 Drawing machine, forest of imagination

■ ■ ■ ■ ART PROCESSES AND PRACTICES

Papers

Children need to experience papers in a wide range of sizes, colours, textures and qualities.

cartridge paper: pencil, charcoal, conte crayon, ink, biro, and felt tips

sugar paper: soft pastel, oil pastel, charcoal, chalk, and wax crayon

Once children are familiar with each medium they can then choose the most appropriate tool and surface for the task in hand. Materials need to be readily available in the classroom and accessible to the children.

Resourcing drawing in the classroom

Good drawing requires a classroom environment conducive to the activity. This means that the teacher needs to provide a range of visual stimuli, objects to provoke observation, discussion, involvement and discrimination.

natural objects (e.g., plants, seeds, pods, bark, stones, shells, fossils, and feathers)

made objects (e.g., cogs, bottles, tools, toys, machinery, ceramics, and artefacts)

Observational drawing

Learning to look, to see more and find meaning, is one of the purposes of working from observation. Children need to be taught the variety of ways in which they can approach their drawings in order to employ the relevant drawing system. Children can build on their previous experience of mark-making and select appropriate paper, drawing media and viewpoint.

Using a viewfinder

Visual analysis is aided by enclosure. Using a paper or cardboard frame will make it easier for children to select and focus their looking just as a photographer uses the

■ **Figure 2.8** Reception, playing with mark-making, shapes and patterns

ART PROCESSES AND PRACTICES

viewfinder of a camera. A viewfinder can be used to compose a picture by selecting part of a 'view' or used to isolate objects or parts of objects. Viewfinders, magnifying glasses and mirrors are all devices which will help to focus attention and encourage children to look carefully.

Focusing children's looking

Looking carefully at objects and situations and discussing them in detail is an important way of focusing children's attention before, during and after drawing. The dialogue between the teacher and the child is often crucial in that it can provide key objectives for the children's learning. When drawing from observation it may be appropriate to focus attention on a particular element within the object of situation such as colour, shape, pattern or texture.

Children need to recognise and appreciate that observational drawing can be done for different reasons. It can be a means of gathering information which can be used to inform a further piece of work, it may be annotated or it can be done for its own sake to find out about the object or situation being drawn. Observational drawing allows children to respond directly to first-hand experience and provides a resource for developing new ideas.

Suggested activities with children (and colleagues!)

Choose an object/artefact to investigate through a series of observational drawings:

alternate looking with mark-making to represent what is seen (e.g., look, draw, look, draw).
draw the object with a continuous line.
draw without looking at the paper, only at the object.
feel the object with your eyes closed and draw your response.
draw with your non-dominant hand.
draw the object from different viewpoints.
focus in on part of the object and draw this in detail.
enlarge your drawings using a magnifying glass.
focus on the colour of the object and make a colour study.
focus on the pattern and texture of the object and record this.
focus on the shape of the object and draw the shape around it.
focus on the dark and light areas and make a tonal study.
analyse the object and annotate your drawing.
draw the object from memory.
describe the object to someone else and ask them to draw it unseen.
draw the reflection of the object in the mirror.
look at artists' observational drawings.

Expressive drawing

This type of drawing allows children to express what they know, feel and imagine. Materials, lines, patterns and colours all have expressive qualities which can provide

ART PROCESSES AND PRACTICES

symbols for our experience. Children need to be able to explore the potential of mark-making and build an understanding of these qualities in order that they can use them in their own work. Looking at other artists' use of expression and emotion in their work is a valuable starting point for children's own art making. Children need to be encouraged to make a personal response to their world and to communicate their feelings about their experiences.

Figure 2.9 Drawing using pastels and ink wash, Year 1

Suggested activities with children (and colleagues!)

Explore materials for their expressive qualities.
Find visual equivalents to words (e.g., soft, hard and spiky).
Explore the range of mark-making possibilities and colours to represent a particular mood or emotion (e.g., excited, calm and angry).
Listen to a piece of music and respond using appropriate media.
Use poetry as a stimulus for drawing.
Describe a personal and meaningful experience through mark-making.
Describe an aspect of your personality by using symbols and colours.
Make exaggerated and distorted drawings of faces to express emotions.
Respond to the elements using appropriate colours and shapes.
Record patterns in movement and dance.
Make a personal statement about a social or political issue using symbols and words.

Narrative drawing

Children have a tremendous capacity to tell visual stories that are both real and imagined. This involves recalling their past experiences as well as fantasising about possibilities. This rich fantasy world is fed by the media and story books, but needs to be encouraged and developed. A wide variety of stimuli should be provided which will

ART PROCESSES AND PRACTICES

feed and extend children's imaginations. Providing children with first hand experiences of visits to places, local events and visitors to school will encourage children to make direct personal responses and record these in their work. Role-play and drama can be valuable tools for initiating imaginary stories. In order to tell imaginative visual stories effectively, children will need to gather and use a wide variety of visual resources to inform their work.

> **Suggested activities with children (and colleagues!)**
>
> Make a memory map to represent a journey, real or imagined.
> Record your visit to the local park, using a story board.
> Invent a character and record visually his/her/its traits.
> Translate an ordinary everyday object into the fantastic.
> Recall a particular event and summarise through drawing.
> Look at artists' use of story, myth and legend.

Illustration

This kind of drawing helps to convey information about the world in which we live. It can be a diagram or a visual account. It helps children to use signs and symbols as evidence of their experience. Illustration may support topic work that children are involved with and can be an integral activity rather than merely servicing other curriculum areas. Children need to be given the opportunity to describe and explain their understanding visually, possibly with annotations. They can describe through drawing how things are made or how things fit together.

> **Suggested activities with children (and colleagues!)**
>
> Describe a process or sequence (e.g., the change from a tadpole into a frog).
> Illustrate stories that you have written yourself.
> Draw maps and plans to illustrate your local environment.
> Make posters and signs for the school community.
> Draw a family tree.
> Draw a diagram to show how a Lego model fits together.

Design

Children should be helped to understand that a drawing is a way of thinking, through which an idea can be explored and developed. They can be encouraged to make rough draft drawings to try out ideas before developing into a finished piece of work. Developing ideas through drawing can also be a useful tool in planning a piece of work as well as recording the outcome. Drawing from observation can be a good starting point for this type of activity as it allows children to gather information from first-hand experience and provides a resource through which they can speculate on

■ ■ ■ ■ **ART PROCESSES AND PRACTICES**

new ideas. At various stages in a design drawing, the children will have the opportunity to share their ideas with others and make changes where necessary.

Drawing skills Tools and media	Processes	Artists' methods	Formal elements
Exploring a range of tools and mark-making materials	Drawing from experience, observation, memory and imagination	Looking at and talking about their own work and the work of others	Exploring elements of line, tone, colour, form, space, pattern, texture and shape
Experimenting with different drawing tools to achieve a variety of qualities	Selecting subject matter and media with increasing independence	Using drawing for different purposes	Experimenting with the visual elements and choosing appropriate media
Using tools safely and looking after materials	Drawing from a range of stimuli	Making connections between their own work and the work of artists	Evaluating and reviewing their own and others' use of the visual and tactile elements
Using a range of paper sizes and their purpose	Collecting and recording visual information as part of a project	Developing knowledge of artists from the past, present and different cultures	Developing a technical and descriptive vocabulary
Using dry media to mix and blend colours	Drawing for sustained periods of time from the figure and real objects	Collecting images and information about a variety of artists drawings and processes	Experimenting with visual and tactile elements in different materials and on a variety of scales
Developing differing techniques when drawing for different purposes	Drawing from observation, memory and imagination; understanding the visual elements and how to achieve variations in each	Evaluating and reviewing their own and others' work in the light of artists processes	Describing changes to their drawings using an art vocabulary
Using a wide variety of marks with different media, layering different materials	Developing and refining drawings	Using a sketchbook, collecting images and information independently	Manipulating the visual and tactile elements of art to personalise their work

> **Suggested activities with children (and colleagues!)**
>
> Make a drawing from observation and select a part of it to develop into a print.
> Try out several ideas for a design for an artefact.
> Use written and visual information to describe the development of an idea.
> Make visual notes to use for a future piece of work.

ART PROCESSES AND PRACTICES

> **Drawing can help facilitate our ability to**
>
> **A**nalyse
> **B**uild
> **C**ommunicate
> **D**ream
> **E**xplore
> **F**antasise
> **G**enerate ideas
> **H**ypothesise
> **I**magine
> **J**uxtapose
> **K**now
> **L**ook
> **M**ake
> **N**arrate
> **O**bserve
> **P**lay
> **Q**uestion
> **R**eflect
> **S**ymbolise
> **T**ransform
> **U**nderstand
> **V**isualise
> **W**onder
> **X**ray
> **Y**earn
> **Z**?
>
> What words would you use?
>
> Adapted from Adams, E. (2002). *Start drawing!* London: The Campaign for Drawing.

Sketchbooks and visual journals

Sketchbooks should be visual diaries or journals which can be referred to as records of ideas and experiences. Sketchbooks can be used for collecting visual information, whether in the form of drawing, annotated sketches, painting, notes, designs or secondary source material. Essentially sketchbooks should be personal and exploratory and contain a combination of visual and written material. They should reflect the child's interest in their own experiences and discoveries. The sketchbook can provide a useful form of dialogue between the teacher and the child in recording the development of ideas and visual experiences. These can become a valuable personal resource for the development of the children's art making. Ideas can be tried out and developed further in a variety of media.

The term sketchbook is a misnomer in that it is not merely a book of sketches. Teachers may wish to use an alternative name to reinforce the purpose of the book (e.g., a visual journal, visual notebook, visual diary, and design book). This will help to attribute value to the work that is included.

■ ■ ■ ■ **ART PROCESSES AND PRACTICES**

Children will be familiar with keeping draft books for writing or topic work, so the idea of a visual notebook can be related easily. Ideally children should be given the opportunity to use sketchbooks to record their direct experience as well as to extend ideas and explore possibilities. Artists, craftspeople and designers keep sketchbooks as evidence of their developing ideas, collecting relevant source material to inform their work. Giving children access to these is a valuable way of asserting the potential of sketchbooks.

At all stages in their learning, there is an emphasis on children taking increasing responsibility for gathering sources for their work and researching themes for themselves. The sketchbook provides an ideal vehicle for translating visual information into developed pieces of artwork. At the same time the sketchbook becomes an artwork in itself and children should be encouraged to develop a personalised book which reflects their individual personality. The use of sketchbooks will also inform and support other areas of the curriculum. Sketchbooks can be purchased from most art material suppliers or can be made simply from folded paper. Introducing children to book making is a valuable activity which will instil a sense of pride and ownership in their work.

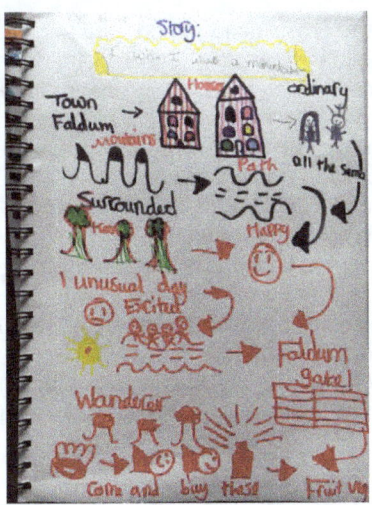

■ **Figure 2.10** Sketchbooks, Year 5, School Without Walls

Sketchbooks can contain

- careful drawings and paintings
- quick sketches in a variety of media
- photographs
- magazine or newspaper cuttings (or both)
- collage ideas
- collections of rubbings

ART PROCESSES AND PRACTICES

- written ideas, sensations and feelings – use all the senses – notes of sounds, smells, temperatures, atmospheres
- experiments with line, tone, colour, pattern, shape/space, and texture
- experiments with working on different surfaces

Suggested activities

Use a **variety of media** to explore **mark-making**.
How many different marks, lines, tones, patterns, textures can you make?
Collect **visual information** about a particular object or place (e.g., the school building and the local environment).
Make **colour notes** or 'swatches', take **rubbings**, draw bits or **fragments**.
Make a **collection** of **cuttings** and **photographs** around a theme (e.g., look at faces in magazines and newspapers).
Using a **viewfinder**, make a series of **observational studies** of natural and made objects (e.g., stones, fossils, shells, bark, cogs, machinery and artefacts).
Focus on one of **visual or tactile elements** (e.g., line, tone, texture, pattern, colour and shape).
Experiment with different media and **mixed media**.
Use your sketchbook to **review** other artists' work, visit an exhibition in a gallery or museum. **Interrogate** the work! Make **personal reflections** on the meaning of the work to you. **Collect** a range of artists' work that you like.
Make a **written commentary** on your work and keep **annotated** sketches.
Find **connections** between the themes and ideas that you are recording.
Make **visual and written lists** about things that interest you. Use your **developing ideas** to inform a **further piece of work**.
Make plans about how you might **develop a sketch** using a different media (e.g., use a photocopier or visualiser to enlarge part of a sketch).
Use the library to do some **research** into a project, **record** your ideas. Write a series of questions which you need to focus on.
Use your sketchbook as a form of **self-assessment**. Talk to your teacher about the areas you feel confident about as well as things you need help with.

A sketchbook assignment

Sensory Walk
Plan to take a walk with activities on the way.
Participants have sketchbooks.
Collect items (work in pairs) – supply bags, choose drawing materials, magnifying glasses, mirrors, and so on.
Four activities on the way – two drawing-based, two word-based.
Walk, observe, sense, collect, draw, write, sort, review, reflect, refine.
Develop ideas in arrange of media.
Materials: bags, drawing, painting, clay, printing, and artists' work

Personal Collections
Focus on past/personal histories/other places.

ART PROCESSES AND PRACTICES

Small groups/pairs: share objects.
Offer a range of possibilities to create a personal box – teacher/child-initiated.
Box to contain artefacts, photos, maps, pictures and so on.
Find suitable relevant artworks.
Box can be guided via particular themes.
Materials: shoeboxes, objects, textiles, drawing, painting, printing, and clay

Figure 2.11 Sketchbook assignment, Year 3

B sketchbook assignment

Colour
Begin with white and add a little primary colour (e.g., red, to make the lightest possible pink).
Paint a patch of this colour in your sketchbook and work in patches from left to right adding more colour each time and finishing with pure primary colour.
Try the same exercise with other primaries or
Mixing two or three primaries to make new colours.
Try giving the colours names – write these in your sketchbook (e.g., sunburst yellow and racing red).
Collect commercial colour charts and cut out interesting colours and names and stick them in your book.
Try colour mixing experiments with

- oil pastels
- powder pastels
- felt tipped pens (e.g., using dots of colour or stripes to create) optical colour mixing
- water colours

Use cut out squares or patches from magazines to create tonal patterns.

ART PROCESSES AND PRACTICES

Colour and painting

Painting involves the child in an exploration of colour and qualities of surface. Gaining an appreciation and sensitivity towards colour is an essential element in each individual's entitlement art curriculum. Children need to work with good tools and materials in painting and to experience and discuss the qualities and potential that particular processes have to offer. In this way, their manual skills will develop and they will be able to select the most appropriate method for their task. Painting as an activity encourages children to develop their ideas, promotes their use of the visual language and forms the basis for personal expression.

Figure 2.12 Painting, Year 1, Batheaston Primary School

There are three fundamental ways of approaching painting activities:

1. As a means of developing children's ideas, impulses, feelings and perceptions. Children will often use painting in direct response to their visual experiences but they also enjoy reorganising their ideas into imaginative forms.
2. Children will also need to learn to control the paint materials and select appropriately from a range of possible approaches.
3. Children will need to develop a clear understanding of the way colours interact in a dynamic way.

Paint systems

There are many different paints available for use in schools – powder colour, ready mixed paint, tempera blocks and watercolour – all provide educational experience and have different advantages. Foundations should be laid at an early age for understanding about colour and best practice is achieved when a school adopts a standard paint

■ ■ ■ ■ **ART PROCESSES AND PRACTICES**

system and range of colours, although it is more important to standardise the range of colours available than the paint medium. The 'double primary colour system' has been developed as the most limited set of colours which will truly provide the full range of colour mixing possibilities. Using this range allows children to experience the subtleties of mixing colours without the additional expense of buying secondary colours.

Practical considerations

To encourage colour mixing, all children should have their own flat palette, a range of brushes, two water pots (one for adding water to the paint and one for cleaning the brush) and a small sponge to remove excess water from their brush. A central tray of powder colours or ready mixed paints can easily be shared. Early paint exploration is purely physical and tactile, this leads to the discovery that paint can be mixed and applied in a variety of ways. Children can use fingers, sticks, sponges, rags, palette knives, feathers as well as brushes to apply the paint. PVA glue, sand and sawdust can each be added to paint to change the texture and consistency. Painting surfaces may include paper, card, textiles or wood.

Paints

Powder colour is probably the best type of paint to teach colour mixing because of the potential for adding very small amounts to make subtle changes to one colour. Paint can be picked up with a damp brush and mixed in patches on a flat palette. Trays of powder paints can easily be organised by purchasing manufactured trays or by using yoghurt pots held in an ice cream container with a lid which can then be stored safely. Good-quality ready mixed paint has the advantage of allowing extensive surface coverage as well as providing the potential for mixing with other media to change the consistency of the paint. Tempera blocks and watercolour blocks are useful for outdoor studies and location work but are not suitable for large-scale work. Children need to experience a range of different paints in order to be discerning in their choices.

Figure 2.13 Painting, Year 2, St Saviour's Infant School

ART PROCESSES AND PRACTICES

Brushes

There should be a selection of brushes available to the children so that the can choose the most appropriate tool for the task. The size and shape of the brush may affect the success of the paint application. It is important to provide a range of fine, medium and thick brushes that are round, flat and pointed. Children need to be encouraged to care and respect these, washing them pointing downwards in running water and to avoid standing them on their bristles.

Paper

The quality of paper used will also determine the response of the paint medium. It is always better to use good-quality paper which will allow the paint to 'sit' properly on the surface. Children need to become aware of the various effects that different surfaces have on the paint, their absorbency, their surface texture and their colour.

Figure 2.14 Using powder paint

Checklist of materials

Ready mixed/powder paint in the double primary system
Range of brushes/tools
Range of papers/surfaces
Two water pots
Sponges
Flat palettes

Paint exploration

Children enjoy the physical experience of using paint, its tactile qualities and the visual effects of different colours. They will develop an increasing control over tools and materials and a growing awareness of the potential for colour mixing and mark-making.

ART PROCESSES AND PRACTICES

PRIMARY COLOURS **BLUE RED YELLOW**
these cannot be obtained by mixing other colours
SECONDARY COLOURS
mixing two primaries
BLUE + RED = **PURPLE**
BLUE + YELLOW = **GREEN**
RED + YELLOW = **ORANGE**
TERTIARY COLOURS RED + BLUE + YELLOW = **BROWN**
mixing all three primaries
ACHROMATIC COLOURS **WHITE GREY BLACK**

Note: The type and quality of paint, the size of brushes, the kinds of paper, the cleanliness of water all make the difference between continued confidence or children's frustration.

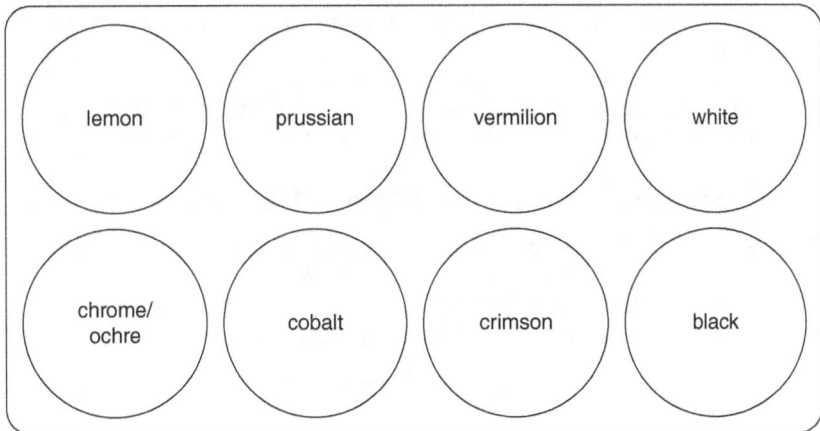

'Pure' primary colours can be mixed from equal quantities of the warm and cold versions of the primary colour. 'Pure' secondary colours can be mixed from appropriate primaries

    orange – chrome yellow and vermilion
    green – lemon yellow and prussian
    purple – crimson and cobalt

Some schools prefer to omit black from the palette to avoid the ubiquitous black outline and a subsequent muddy colour raange! Prussian mixed with vermilion can provide a variety of blacks and a third blue such as turquoise or brilliant blue can be included in the palette.

> **Suggested activities**
>
> Teach children a sequence for mixing paint
>   dip the brush in the water
>   wipe it on the sponge
>   put it in the paint
>   mix in the palette
> Playing with paint to make it thick. thin, wet, dry, smooth, textured, on different surfaces (e.g., card and wet paper)

ART PROCESSES AND PRACTICES

Encourage children to 'test out' colours on strips of paper which can be used to build a colour wheel/chart
Focus on colour mixing to explore:
- a range of one colour (e.g., greens or browns)
- a range of tints or shades (e.g., light blues or dark reds)
- complementary colours (e.g., yellow and purple)
- colour contrasts (e.g., warm and cold)
- colour families (e.g., autumn colours)
- matching colours (e.g., skin colour)

Focus on the consistency of the paint to explore its opaque and translucent qualities on different surfaces.
Explore the potential for building up layers of paint to create depth and distance.
Focus on the application of the paint and the potential for mark-making with different tools.
Collect colour charts from paint manufacturers.
Use sketchbooks to collect resource material and make colour studies.
Look at the work of different artists to understand painting in various times and cultures.

Questions to focus the children's learning

How does the colour of the paint change as it dries?
How does the colour of the surface affect the colour of the paint?
How does the consistency of the paint affect the intensity of the colour?
How does one colour react when placed beside another?

Observational painting

Painting from observation allows children the opportunity to make personal responses to the natural and made world. Developing observational skills and encouraging children to really 'see' is an important element of art and design. Through careful looking children can respond to and communicate their experiences with increasing sensitivity and understanding. There is a close link between drawing and painting although with painting the emphasis is usually on colour and surface. (It is inappropriate to ask a child to make a drawing and then to 'colour it in' with paint!) In painting as in drawing, children will develop the use of a schema to express their observations of their world, moving towards a more objective response and an awareness of the visual world.

Suggested activities

Paint natural and made objects from observation (e.g., stones, bark, shells, plants, fruit, machinery, toys, and artefacts).
Make colour studies of the natural and made environment (e.g., hedgerows, fields, trees, gardens, buildings to develop into a landscape painting).
Paint portraits of their friends or self.
Focus on the texture and pattern of materials and textiles.
Look at different artists' paintings of people, places and objects.
Select a small section of an artists' reproduction to recreate the colour and surface qualities.

■ ■ ■ ■ **ART PROCESSES AND PRACTICES**

■ **Figure 2.15** Observational painting, Year 2

Expressive painting

Through the use of colour and surface children can explore, express and communicate their ideas and feelings. The emotive power of colour and its symbolic use provides a vehicle for expressing complex and subtle meanings. Children make intuitive and immediate responses to colour which can be built on to extend their learning. They will develop an understanding of the relationship between the way the paint is applied, the colours they use and the subject matter they choose to convey.

Suggested activities

Make a painting that describes a particular feeling (e.g., scary, excited and sad).
Consider the colours and the way the paint is applied.
Respond in paint to a chosen poem or piece of music.
Paint a portrait of your friend or yourself which describes their/your personality.
Record your feelings in paint in response to a particular place or event.
Choose an object to paint from observation and look at it in a new way by
- changing its scale
- intensifying its colour
- looking at it in a distorted mirror
- rearranging its composition

Look at the work of the Expressionists to develop an understanding of how different artists have used paint to express ideas and feelings.

ART PROCESSES AND PRACTICES

Narrative painting

Children are able to tell stories through their early paintings often before they can communicate them in writing. The meanings, characters and events will often change and they will continue to rename their images according to their needs. Children will develop an understanding about the potential for using images to convey meanings. Through their paintings they will be able to relate complex stories in a visual form.

> **Suggested activities**
>
> Make a painting that describes a journey you remember.
> Make a painting of an imaginary place or person.
> Make a painting that records a special event.
> Look at paintings from different times and cultures that tell stories.

Illustration

Children's book illustration is a useful starting point for teaching children about illustrative painting. By looking at the use of media, colour, tonal qualities, scale, composition, shape, linear rhythms and symbols, children will be able to apply their understanding to inform their own work.

Planning paintings

Sometimes it is appropriate for children to plan their work. Ideas can be explored and discussed before they start a painting. Using a sketchbook is a useful tool to encourage children to look closely, collect ideas and visual information to inform their

Figure 2.16 Construction, Year 3

paintings. They can make initial colour studies, try out different compositions and develop ideas in a range of media. With this in mind, children can also be encouraged to return to their paintings in progress and develop them further. This will help them become more confident in reviewing and modifying their work, to make necessary changes and develop a more sustained approach to working.

SCULPTURE

Modelling and constructing in three dimensions develop visual, tactile and spatial awareness in children. Children experience their world mainly in three dimensions and it is through an accessible variety of media that they may explore shape, form and texture. It is important that children have the opportunity to engage in a variety of three dimensional work on a regular basis. The value of 3D activities is essential to

- the development of the relationships which exist between form, shape and scale.
- the development of an understanding of the different materials, tools and processes which can be used for modelling and constructing.
- the realisation that different materials offer possibilities for making observations, expressing and interpreting ideas and feelings.

Materials

Clay, plaster, textiles, wire, card, paper, wood, and found forms

What needs to be taught?

- nature and quality of materials
- appropriateness of materials
- use of tools
- constructing and joining techniques
- investigation of space and form, internal and external, positive and negative
- space measurement, weight, strength, force, balance

Skills involved

Designing and thinking through making

Resistant materials: cutting, joining, folding, bending, tearing, interlocking, shaping, measuring, estimating...
Plasticity of materials: modelling, moulding, carving, casting, manipulating, squeezing, prodding, rolling, pushing...

Recyclable materials and containers can form the basis for fruitful artwork. It is important that these materials are grouped and organised and not presented as a pile of 'junk', which may devalue the activity.

ART PROCESSES AND PRACTICES ■ ■ ■ ■

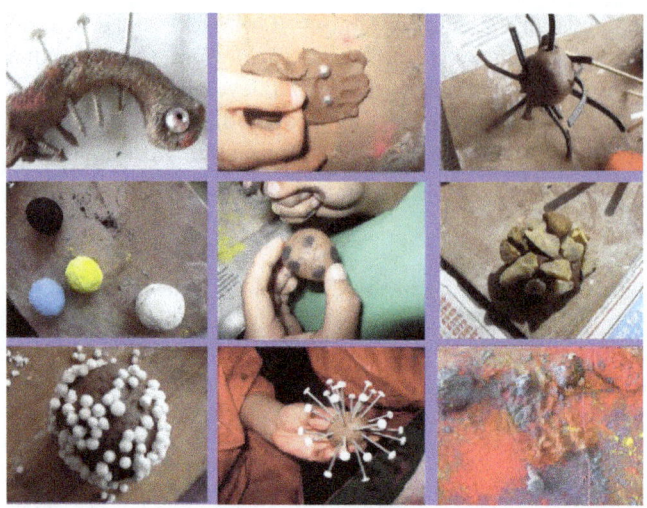

Figure 2.17 Working with Clay, Year 2, St Vigor and St John Primary School, Chilcompton

Working with clay

Clay is one of the most ancient art forms of human history. It is a plastic, malleable material which has unique qualities. Modelling and constructing in three dimensions develop visual, tactile and spatial awareness in children. When children are first introduced to clay, it is essential that they are encouraged to explore the nature of the material through manipulation. This should be focused and guided in such a way as to enable children to discover how to handle the material and find out its potential and limitations.

> How many ways can they discover to change a piece of clay?
> (e.g., pinching, squeezing, prodding, pulling, twisting, rolling, beating, pressing, and tearing)
> How flat can you make the clay before holes start appearing?
> How long a snake or coil can you make before it starts to break?
> How many holes can you make in a ball of clay and still keep its shape?
> How many spikes can you pull from a ball of clay, strong enough to support it without bending or breaking off?

Purposeful exploration and manipulation of clay allows children to develop their confidence in using the material and increase their understanding of its properties and qualities. Activities need to build on this initial exploration in order to develop further skills and techniques.

Younger children are more likely to want to use clay to model their experiences and imagination than make abstract forms or functional objects. The content of their three-dimensional work will be very similar to their paintings and drawings of their immediate world. With this in mind they will want to learn more specific skills to enable them to make figures and the types of objects which they find in their environment. They will need to learn how to pull a figure from a single ball of clay without having to join pieces on. The less joining they have to do, the stronger the model will be.

Children need to be taught three basic modelling and constructing techniques which can be adapted to their individual projects.

Hollow forms (thumb pots)
Coiling
Slabbing

Hollow forms
Supporting a ball of clay in your cupped hand, gradually press out a hole with the thumb of your other hand, gently turning the clay and squeezing between your thumb and fingers. Smooth out the pot until it is no thinner than 1/2 cm and semi-spherical in shape. Flatten out the rim by gently tapping on the table.

Coiling
Practise hand rolling coils, trying to keep the pressure of your fingers equal to obtain an even coil. Practise making a coil pot by building on the base of a thumb pot. Smooth the coils so that they are worked together on either the inner or outer sides of the pot.

Slabbing
Roll out a slab of clay between two slats placed either side of the clay on a porous surface (e.g., card, wood or cloth). The clay needs to be roughly manipulated towards the size and shape of the slab needed. The thickness of the slats will determine the thickness of the slab. Use a wooden rolling pin to avoid sticking, turning the clay around and over to allow the clay to expand. Leave the clay to go leather-hard so that it can be used to construct forms or wrap round formers (e.g., cardboard tubes). (Use newspaper to prevent the clay from sticking to the former and remove both before the clay shrinks as it loses moisture.) Use **slip** (clay and water paste) to join the clay.

Surface decoration
Mark-making in clay encourages children to explore pattern, texture and surface qualities. Use a variety of found and made tools to push into the clay and pull out the surface.

Carving
Children can 'bang out' three dimensional shapes of clay on the table top or wooden board, leave these to go leather hard and carve. Clay to be fired must be hollowed out.

Colouring clay
Painting onto the surface of fired or air dried clay is possible with ordinary classroom paints such as powder or ready mix. The painted object can be varnished with matt, silk of polyurethane varnish depending on the surface quality required. There are also coloured oxides, slips and glazes available if clay is to be fired.

ART PROCESSES AND PRACTICES

Classroom organisation

One of the most important tasks for the teacher is to always present the children with clay in a manageable condition. Clay is best worked when it is soft and malleable but not sticky. In this **plastic** state, it can be joined, will retain marks and impressions and has a certain amount of structural strength, if not modelled too thinly. As it dries, it becomes **leather hard**, more rigid and stronger, but less easy to bend and mould. In this state, it can be carved. When clay is completely dry, or **green**, it is rigid but easily broken. When fired in a kiln, it changes its chemical structure and becomes progressively harder, the higher the temperature. In its sticky state, **slip**, it can be used to join soft and leather hard clay together.

Clay can be stored in an air tight container in manageable sized balls and covered with a damp cloth and a plastic sheet. Children can then easily access the clay and work on a wooden board or a piece of card or cloth. They can keep their hands cool and moist by pressing them on damp sponges at intervals while they work. At the end of a session, the children can reconstitute the used clay into balls and put them back in the bin for re-use. It is not essential that every activity should have a finished product, even when a kiln is available it is not necessary to fire everything. It is far more important that children have the opportunity to handle the material often, play, build, model explore and learn to reprocess, than to make finished pieces. Children need to learn to appraise their work critically and understand that each outcome is part of an ongoing process.

Printmaking, collage and textiles

Activity: Exploring printmaking

Make a collection of patterns from different cultures: Islamic, Celtic, African, Asian, Aztec and Aboriginal art are useful sources to choose from. Invite the children to use their sketchbooks to collect a range of different patterns. Choose appropriate drawing media which will help them **explore the qualities of the patterns,** for example, soft pencils, black felt-tips or biros. Discuss the range of patterns and their meanings. Encourage them to **invent their own patterns** using these as a starting point.

Ask the children to select one of the patterns to enlarge onto a print block: use dense polystyrene printing tiles, card or string to make the block. It may be useful to spend some time exploring a variety of different print methods before the children select an appropriate one. Discuss the surface of the block and the use of pattern and space before the children ink up the block. Use a single colour initially, preferably black so that the focus remains on pattern rather than colour at this point.

Encourage the children to take a series of prints to explore the range of effects they can make with varying amounts of ink and pressure.

Invite the children to develop their printmaking by making a series of repeated prints; rotating the block to develop a design; changing the colour of the ink or the paper or both; adding more detail to the print or taking away some detail and then overprinting one colour onto another. Each child could include their print as part of a whole class design on a large sheet of paper: this will obviously have implications for the size of the blocks that you give to the children.

Discuss the finished prints and make a whole class display. Any prints left over could form the basis for a collage or you could encourage the children to draw back into them with mixed media.

■ ■ ■ ■ **ART PROCESSES AND PRACTICES**

To ensure less mess when organising printmaking, encourage the children to keep all their printing equipment on a printing 'island' (an A3 newspaper) and use a magazine to print on, turning to a clean page each time a new print is taken.

You can take any shape or line and play with it by photocopying it and enlarging it, reversing it, inverting it, repeating it, cutting it up and changing it (take a face from a colour supplement and cut it vertically into strips. Then re-order the face from right to left, or from top to bottom, or both).

Resources

Water-based printing inks, rollers, inking trays, poly-printing tiles, card or string, glue, scissors, a range of papers, and a collection of patterns from different cultures.

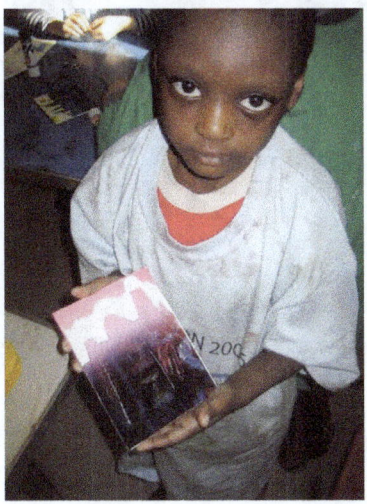

■ **Figure 2.18** Printmaking, Year 3

Activity: Exploring collage and textiles

Offer children a wide range of collage materials to experiment with including a variety of papers (tissue, crepe, cellophane and foils), stickers, tape, feathers, leaves, seeds, sticks, shapes, bottle tops, buttons, fabric, wool and string.

Use a range of **natural, recycled plastic, metal or fabric** and so on to create a themed collage, encouraging children to think about colour and texture, by layering, combining and twisting materials. Introduce basic weaving techniques, talking about the process of warp and weft.

Use threading templates, pieces of recycled plastic mesh for children to practise technique of weaving using strips of material. Make paper weavings using coloured paper or card.

Introduce and practise basic stitching on binca/hessian/felt as decoration but also as a means of joining materials. Introduce fabric crayon, paints and markers. Use these skills and techniques to create a mixed media fabric collage.

ART PROCESSES AND PRACTICES

> Using stitching as a decorative technique on top of fabric drawing or painting, to add detail. Create woven or mixed media structures. Opportunities for children to demonstrate a range of skills. Use collage as a different type of drawing, to express ideas. Look at early cubist work (e.g., Braque's Picasso Gris, also Kurt Schwitters).
>
> Produce an abstract picture from the exploration of a collection of every day images – these should be of individual interest to each child.

Figure 2.19 Using collage, Year 4, School Without Walls

Digital art

Digital processes can be integrated into an art activity as both a support and as a medium in itself. All classrooms should have access to a computer, tablets and corresponding programmes, whether these are specifically art-based depends on the software available. It is important for teachers to become familiar with the nature and variety of programmes in order to select the most appropriate one for the task. Children can be encouraged to use the computer as a drawing, painting or printing medium, exploring mark-making, line and colour, just as they might with graphic or liquid media. The computer can be used extensively for observational drawing, offering an alternative means of recording children's responses. The screen can be used for drafting ideas, designing using images and text, pattern making incorporating colour and line.

The quality of colour on the screen is unnatural and needs to be compared with the actual colours produced by the printer. The advantage of exploring colours on the screen is the speed at which colours can be changed, as well as the potential for exploring spatial and expressive effects. The image has a stepped 'pixel' structure like the dots on a television screen, this can be zoomed into in order to make adjustments to small areas of the image.

Innovative computer technology will allow children to research art and use them as a resource for their developing work. Digital art provides a highly interactive medium for both individual and collaborative work, offering children endless possibilities for developing ideas. Children with special needs can often make positive achievements through computer aided design.

■ ■ ■ ■ **ART PROCESSES AND PRACTICES**

> **Digital art: Suggested activities**
>
> Experimenting
> Mark-making
> Drafting ideas
> Diagrams
> Freehand drawing
> Manipulation of images
> Colour arrangement
> Composition and layout
> Zooming in on images
> Lettering
> Pattern exploration
> Editing

CHAPTER SUMMARY

This chapter has given an overview of the processes and practices in the art and design curriculum, including the practical, critical and cultural aspects of learning in the visual arts. The importance of direct experience of different art processes alongside the dialogue with children about their own and others' artwork is vital in developing understanding in art and design.

REFERENCES AND FURTHER READING

Craft, A. (2001) Little c Creativity. In A. Craft, B. Jeffrey and M. Leibling (Eds.), *Creativity in Education* (pp. 45–61). London: Continuum.

Gude, O. (2007) Principles of Possibility: Considerations for a 21st Century Art and Culture Curriculum. *Art Education*, 60 (1), 6–17.

Heath, S. B. (2000) Seeing Our Way into Learning. *Cambridge Journal of Education*, 30 (1), 121–132.

Jeffrey, B. and Craft, A. (2006) Creative Learning and Possibility Thinking. In B. Jeffrey (Ed.), *Creative Learning Practices: European Experiences* (pp. 73–91). London: Tufnell Press.

Raney, K. (1999) Visual Literacy and the Art Curriculum. *Journal of Art and Design Education*, 18 (1), 34–47.

SUGGESTED WEBSITES

ENGAGE (UK) National Association for Gallery Education. http://www.engage.org/home/index.aspx
http://www.thebigdraw.org/the-campaign-for-drawing
http://www.drawing-research-network.org.uk/

CHAPTER 3

CONTEMPORARY ART AND CHILDREN'S ART

Among the aims of this book are to help children to be able to identify as artists from an early age, to understand the processes involved and to become immune to the potentially negative experience of 'school art' as being different from contemporary art practice (Reiss and Pringle 2003). This chapter explores a contemporary and innovative approach to visual arts education, informed by relevant theories, with examples of practice and relevant case studies. The chapter draws on evidence of collaboration between artists and children as a significant and legitimate learning process, demonstrating how work with children can be central for many artists and is becoming increasingly respected as a field of practice.

Discussion will include the following:

- the problem with a National Curriculum
- the value of art in children's lives
- working with contemporary art and artists
- working with galleries and art museums
- using children's book illustrations
- popular and contemporary culture
- contemporary art in different cultures

Throughout this book, emphasis is placed on encouraging teachers to provide a framework of activities within which children can place their own experiences and question the nature of art and design

- to support teaching and learning in art and design with specific reference to responding to the work of contemporary artists to inform pupils' own work
- to encourage multiple readings of artists' work and to value individual responses
- to introduce examples of young artists' work as well as work of more well-known artists
- to develop understanding of the ways that contemporary art embodies and reflects the issues and concerns of society

- to place art and design in its historical, social and cultural context
- to use art and design for studying similarities, inter-connections and differences between the way people think and feel

THE PROBLEM WITH A NATIONAL CURRICULUM

Since the introduction of a National Curriculum in England, central government policy in education has restricted learning by focusing too much on prescribed knowledge and its assessment. In recent years, schooling has been focused primarily on the transmission of knowledge and skills. 'Traditional' notions of teaching visual art prioritise a deficit or transmission model of learning that is prescriptive. Traditional models of 'school art' may offer little educational or artistic value if the learning is already pre-defined by adults (often denigrated to pre-made models or stencils), as prescribed by a National Curriculum.

The 2014 English National Curriculum for Art and Design consists of a minimal set of guidance for teachers: a two-page document that does not describe the unique nature, depth, breadth and future of the subject and does not demonstrate the value of art in children's lives today. The document sets out the content to use a range of materials; to use drawing, painting and sculpture; to share ideas, experiences and imagination; to develop and become proficient in the use of colour, pattern, texture, line, shape, form and space; to learn about the work of artists, craftspeople and designers; and to use sketchbooks. Such minimalism may be liberating to those who prefer the flexibility to design their own content, but will be a matter of concern to those lacking in confidence and resorting to pre-designed and prescriptive units of work.

Despite some highly creative work existing in pockets, there is a crisis of confidence, particularly within primary art education, perhaps attributable to a more complex range of conditions and circumstances. These include the status of the arts in education with commensurate limitations of time and resources, a lack of provision for professional development, the demise of local authorities and a lack of a critical framework to understand and recognise the benefits engendered.

One of the current orthodoxies in art education is seeing art as an acquisition of skills and competencies a deficit model of learning which characterises children as lacking in abilities and skills and in need of support from an adult to reach a preconceived outcome. Such an adult removes the child's own potentiality as an artist. This indicates the space to explore alternatives to the prevailing doctrine and present more case studies of current pedagogical practice with creativity at the centre.

THE VALUE OF ART IN CHILDREN'S LIVES

To counter this, we need to show the value of art in children's lives and to empower teachers in relation to their own creative capacities, enabling them to co-design and facilitate creative interventions and simultaneously be able to construct a rationale for them. An artist is an individual who engages with ideas about their experience, thoughts and feelings and expresses these in a chosen medium to construct meaning. As teachers, we need to take children's ideas seriously and support children in the exploration and expression of their ideas in a 'hundred languages' (Edwards *et al.* 1998). Before the age

CONTEMPORARY ART AND CHILDREN'S ART

Figure 3.1 Children's expression in 100 languages, Freshford Primary School

of six, children's brains are particularly receptive and adaptable. In this sense, children are researchers, as artists are researchers (Bancroft *et al.* 2008).

The world of art, craft and design offers endless inspiration for creative teaching and learning in art and across the wider curriculum. Contemporary art is particularly relevant to children as they are living 'in the now'. Children can learn about the work of a range of artists, craft makers and designers, describing the differences and similarities between different practices and disciplines and making links to their own work.

The role of art is vital in children's learning about the world around them and in their coming to terms with their own personal role or identity within the cultures in which they are growing up. Children use art both as a way of telling others what matters to them and as a way of exploring new ideas, concepts and emotions for themselves. Often, the narratives they create in artwork are paralleled by their oral storying and role-play. Children move fluently from one mode of representation to another, often using play as the vehicle for their explorations of how to represent and re-represent what they know.

HABITS OF MIND

House of Imagination research has previously identified learning dispositions and 'habits of mind' that have been observed when children are engaged in rich and deep ways. These included, for example, playfulness, imagination, initiating their own ideas, making connections, negotiating, resilience and persistence. Thorough documentation of their thoughts, feelings and ideas forms the basis of creative learning, and responsive planning is used to develop and pursue further ideas. In this context, the artist is seen as a creative enabler and facilitator of possibilities. The role of the artist is to enable, facilitate, collaborate and co-research with children.

■ ■ ■ ■ **CONTEMPORARY ART AND CHILDREN'S ART**

Once children are helped to perceive themselves as authors or inventors, once they are helped to discover the pleasures of inquiry, their motivation and interest explode ... to disappoint the children deprives them of possibilities that no exhortation can arouse in later years.

(Edwards *et al.* 1998)

Habits of mind and creative dispositions, together with skills and attitudes, are central to artistic inquiry, particularly in relation to the role of imagination. The Studio Thinking Framework from Project Zero involves eight studio habits of mind – understanding artwork, developing craft, stretch and explore, engage and

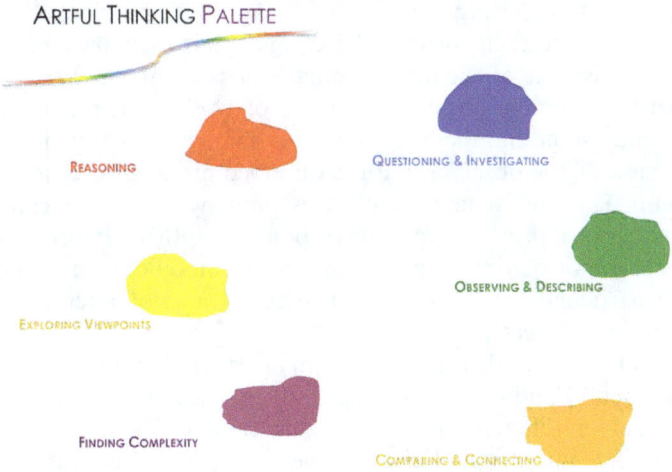

■ **Figure 3.2** The Artful Thinking Palette, Project Zero, Harvard University

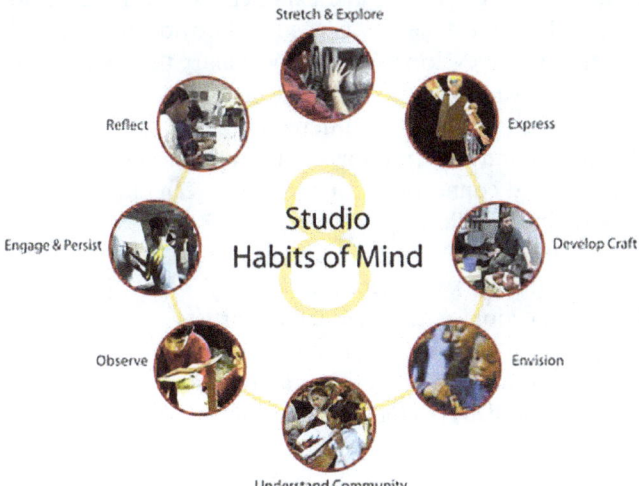

■ **Figure 3.3** Studio Habits of Mind, Project Zero, Harvard University

CONTEMPORARY ART AND CHILDREN'S ART

persist, reflect, envision, observe and express. Comprising skills, inclinations and alertness to opportunities, the studio habits of mind reflect particular creative learning processes and offer the potential to link and connect ideas.

Art can foster children's construction of their own knowledge and the development of creative skills, such as higher-level thinking, analytical ability, problem solving, reflexive thinking and self-regulation.

THE VALUE OF USING CONTEMPORARY ART

Using contemporary art with children allows them to explore their experiences of the world in relation to practising artists who are dealing with cross-cultural issues, the 'here and now'. Using the work of living artists provides the means by which children can relate their ideas and feelings about their own personal, social and cultural worlds. One of the most important aspects of looking at art is the experience that the individual brings to a piece of work to help make connections and develop understanding; there is a need for some kind of relationship between the existing view of the observer and the observed piece in order to make the looking purposeful. This involvement encourages empathy and the development of a sensitivity to their own responses and the responses of others. It also provides a stimulus for the exploration of ideas, concepts and values embodied in the work. Contemporary work, in particular, provides children with a frame of reference within which to place their experiences.

Providing an entitlement curriculum in art, craft and design necessitates the use of contemporary and historical work, work by men and women from different cultures, made for different purposes, in different contexts and in different styles. Although contemporary art is made in the present and often is about current issues, it also helps children to understand the past and to anticipate the future. Using contemporary work helps children to challenge preconceptions about the way things are in order to imagine how things could be. Contemporary art is inevitably going to relate to some of the interests, concerns and experiences of children growing up in a diverse society. Essentially, as teachers, we need to provide opportunities for children to engage with art and to develop a critical vocabulary through which to share ideas with others about their own work and the work of others.

Teaching creatively involves different ways of encouraging children to participate in the process and construction of interpretation of contemporary work in art and design. Practical connections are made between children's work and contemporary art practice in the following ways:

- focusing on the work of selected artists
- making connections with other art and artists
- working directly from children's own interests
- using discussion-based and critical activities
- looking at how ideas change and develop

CONTEMPORARY ART AND CHILDREN'S ART

WORKING WITH CONTEMPORARY ARTISTS

Research has shown that artists can be effective role models for children in dealing with powerful and complex ideas. Creating a shared language to investigate how collaboration with artists can support children in the generation of these ideas is an important aspect of a new learning culture that values children and allows them to engage in these processes. Contemporary art education practices may best be served by shifting the focus from the formal art classroom to a space between the school and the realms of contemporary art and popular culture meet, to allow for movement between the content of the classroom and the contemporary contexts from which children draw their interests.

In the spirit of the Reggio Emilia approach (Edwards *et al.* 1998), the development of ideas often depends on the social interaction of group reflections and conversations. Drawing on their own skills and dispositions, artists can offer possible structures or 'holding forms' for children's expressivity. Documentation in relation to this process is vital in revealing children's fascinations and curiosities. So, too, is provocation or intervention. In response to children's ideas, artists can offer pivotal moments to extend children's ideas. This process requires a culture of open discussion about creative processes and about the notion of being an artist (Vecchi 2010).

House of Imagination (formerly *5x5x5=creativity*) encourages adults and children to be researchers of the world, exploring creative ideas. The commitment to working as an artist or as a creative facilitator necessitates developing professionalism in this area. This involves offering personal skills and modelling creative dispositions with children as well as developing enabling contexts in which the children can develop their own interests and express ideas. The emphasis in both the Reggio Emilia approach and *House of Imagination* is on the artist as a creative enabler, who works alongside children in the thinking process.

Figure 3.4 Exploring Yoyoi Kusama's Polka Dots installation, Year 4

CONTEMPORARY ART AND CHILDREN'S ART

CHILDREN WORKING AS ARTISTS

For children, working as artists allows them to explore their own ideas and see how they can be developed by exploring contemporary art practice in conversation with others, asking good questions, making sense, understanding and developing work in a supportive environment and a creative space. Careful observations of children and close documentation of their work has provided an insight into their interests and fascinations. The adults facilitated and supported the children's depth of learning by respecting these individual interests and by taking time to make connections with the children's thinking. Underpinning this approach is the emphasis on supporting children's developing ideas, thoughts and feelings. Children have opportunities for exploration and response, and there is an emphasis on using innovative and imaginative approaches that stimulate the imagination and encourage independent thought.

Figure 3.5 Children visiting the Black Swan Gallery, Frome

VISITING A GALLERY

A visit to a gallery is an exciting and meaningful way to engage children in looking at and talking about different types of art, craft and design, experiencing work made in different contexts, for different purposes and by men and women from different times and cultures. Visual art exhibitions can provide children with a rich and varied resource with which to develop their own understanding of the world they live in.

Listed below are examples of questions which may help to focus thinking about exhibitions:

CONTEMPORARY ART AND CHILDREN'S ART

What do you expect in an art gallery?
What is actually in the gallery?
What do people do in a gallery?
What do you do?
What materials do artists use?
What materials have been used in this exhibition?
What is the exhibition about?
What do you think the artist is telling us?
Which piece made you think?
Which piece puzzled you?
What value does the work have?
To the artist? To you?

These suggested activities highlight the need for some kind of relationship to be made between the personal experience of the child and the artwork, in order to make the looking purposeful:

OTHER STARTING POINTS

Invite the children to focus on one or more of the following processes:

- collecting images
- collecting words
- exploring issues
- using materials
- expressing feelings
- telling a story

Activity: Why not set up a 'children's gallery' in your school or local centre? The children could be responsible for the content of the changing exhibitions, the curation, the invigilation, the publicity and the signage. Keep an eye out for local and national galleries and museums as well as touring exhibitions.

Activity for colleagues

Using children's book illustrations

Why?

- illustrations provide children with an affective visual experience of storying
- images aid language and literacy development
- expressive powers of images enable books to function as art objects stimulating personal responses

CONTEMPORARY ART AND CHILDREN'S ART

- images give form to ideas and contribute to children's aesthetic development
- images can represent real or imaginary worlds
- images reflect the values of the society and times that produce and use them
- illustrations can be used as a reference point for children's own experience
- illustrations provide a history of style and form
- illustrations provide a visual metaphor for concepts which cannot be easily expressed in words

Ways of analysing an illustration: focus on one or more of the following

media	composition
colour scheme	shape
tonal qualities	linear rhythms
scale	symbols

In order to benefit fully from the richness of visual information, children need to be introduced to the processes involved in reading images. As teachers, we need to be open-minded to the possibilities that illustrations provide for children to make meaning of the printed word. Illustrations can act as a diagrammatic interpretation of the text as well as existing as an art form in their own right. They carry meanings which are personal, cultural and unique to each book. Encourage children to look, search, reflect and interpret.

Suggested activities

- analysing and deconstructing children's book illustrations: Who makes the magic? The author, the illustrator, the reader?
- looking at the relationship between image and text: reading text, reading images – Do they tell the same story? How does the text relate to the images? Are there any visual clues to interpreting the text?
- analysing books in terms of presentation (e.g., cover, quality of paper, size, text, dispersion of images, relationship between text and illustrations, use of colour, font, spacing, layout, frame, continuity and viewpoints).
- looking at different styles of handwriting and print in relation to the history of writing.
- researching the history of paper, the process of making paper and the use of paper (e.g., wrapping, wallpaper and postal communication).
- looking at artists' work, interpreting images and imagining new possibilities, drafting ideas for extra illustrations.

Art experiences, aside from helping to develop children's expression, help to develop their literacy, numeracy and writing skills. Drawing and painting reinforce motor skills and can also be a way of learning about shapes, contrasts, boundaries, spatial relationships, size and other mathematical concepts. Providing an opportunity for children to work with artists, craftspeople and designers is an excellent way of enriching the art and design curriculum.

SUMMARY

Working with artists and contemporary art brings the following benefits to both children and teachers:

- insight into the professional work of an artist
- opportunity to work alongside another adult
- building confidence in art and design
- learning new skills and techniques
- increased awareness of art forms
- breakdown stereotypes about what 'art' is
- heightening interest and participation in art
- raising awareness of the value of art
- developing cross-curricular links

REFERENCES AND FURTHER READING

Bancroft, S., Fawcett, M., and Hay, P. (2008) *Researching Children Researching the World: 5x5x5=creativity*. Stoke-on-Trent, UK: Trentham Books.

Edwards, C., Gandini, L., and Forman, G. (1998) *The Hundred Languages of Children: The Reggio Emilia Approach—Advanced Reflections*. Greenwich, CT: Ablex Publishing.

Reiss, V. and Pringle, E. (2003) The Role of Artists in Sites for Learning. *International Journal of Art & Design Education*, 22 (2), 215–221.

Vecchi, V. (2010) *Art and Creativity in Reggio Emilia: Exploring the Role and Potential of Ateliers in Early Childhood Education*. London: Routledge.

CHAPTER 4
CASE STUDIES

This chapter will offer case studies to involve children in art-making creatively and will illustrate the potential of teaching art creatively through the creative involvement of the teacher in developing children's artistic capability and creative competencies. Innovative case studies will focus particularly on artists in education settings and the concept of children as artists. These case studies will offer the opportunity to explore the adult–child relationships and particularly examine the focus on the role of the adult in supporting children's creative development and identity as artists.

'BEING AN ARTIST'

A strand of my own work is my role as an artist and parent, working with children at a local primary school. With artist Jane Turner, I co-designed the concept of 'Being an Artist' workshops to extend the opportunities for children's art-making and to give them the experience of working as artists, alongside other artists. The aim of 'Being an Artist' is to go beyond the given curriculum and allow the children considerable freedom to express themselves through different processes and media in the visual arts, in a designated creative space. 'Being an Artist' allows children to explore their own ideas and how they can be developed. It involves exploring art practice in conversation with others, asking good questions, making sense of experience, making meaning, and understanding and developing work in a supportive environment.

Key questions asked of the children during 'Being an Artist' workshops are 'What do you want to say through your art?' and 'How do you want to share your ideas with others?' Through these workshops, children have opportunities for exploration and for response and contextualisation of artwork, with emphasis on using innovative and imaginative approaches that stimulate the imagination and encourage independent thought.

The emphasis in the workshops is on different ways of knowing and thinking about art (and life): intuitive, practical, expressive and intellectual. Through dialogue, we explore ideas about being an artist and how ideas are generated and developed. Emphasis on the children's independence, autonomy and freedom to choose both themes and materials to explore contrasts with the Reggio Emilia approach, where the children's theories and fascinations are supported in a co-constructed enquiry.

In 'Being an Artist' workshops, each child has a sketchbook (visual journal or ideas book) that is personalised. This journal also aids my own reflections on the children's learning and has informed my thinking in relation to their developing self-image as artists. Children soon take responsibility for developing their own ideas and themes in their own work, in the context of the group. Each workshop session, children are encouraged to choose what they want to do and to work at their own pace so that they have a natural and personal experience of being an artist. 'Children need to be taught some skills, they will know others, they will have fun and pleasure, ownership of the project and a sense of well-being' (Laevers 2015). In this context, careful observations of children provide an insight into their interests and preoccupations. The adults facilitate and support the children's ideas by respecting individual interests and taking time to make connections with the children's thinking. Underpinning this approach is the emphasis on supporting children's developing ideas, thoughts and feelings.

I focused on the children's art-making, their dialogue and response to questions; I listened to interactions among children as they made art. I noted how they used materials, developed ideas and shared their artwork with me and with each other. I returned to a set of generic questions that were used in response to the situation at the time. These included 'What are your ideas?', 'How do you want to share your ideas?', and 'Where have your ideas come from?' These open-ended questions were intended to get a discussion going among the children, so that they would be responding not only to me but to each other.

Emphasis was on their developing understanding of the concept of being an artist, understanding of their own processes in art-making, what it meant to them, and what the experience was like for them. Children were invited to tell the story of how they created something and how they made certain decisions along the way.

At age 7, Lily shared her thoughts with me about being an artist:

> It's easy!
> Have a great imagination, and then you will have great ideas
> be positive, don't worry if you make mistakes
> be good at playing
> be good at thinking, be thoughtful
> art is about everything!

These comments informed my developing interest in how children can reach a clear sense of their own identity and competency as creative beings and as artists.

I invited Lily to share her thoughts with other children (ages 4–11 years) at Batheaston Primary School, who talked about Lily's ideas and offered their own:

Thea: 'It is about being free, free as a bird.'
Billy: 'You can make anything you want to, it's up to you.'
Ben: 'Art is fun, I love being an artist.'
Charlie: 'You can choose what you do.'
Hannah: 'You can always have something up your sleeve if you're stuck.'

CASE STUDIES

Lily continued to discuss the children's thoughts about being an artist and her own concept of being an 'expert' in something that is valued for its own sake. The concept of 'Being an Artist' is openly discussed and valued, both in the context of the research with $5 \times 5 \times 5 = creativity$ and in relation to the school's ethos.

HOUSE OF IMAGINATION (FORMERLY 5 × 5 × 5 = CREATIVITY): BATHEASTON PRIMARY SCHOOL

Edwina Bridgeman is a visual artist who uses found materials to transform and tell stories. With the main research question of 'Where do ideas come from?,' the children visited Edwina's exhibition at the Victoria Art Gallery in Bath. The theme was 'Shelter' and with the children Edwina shared her ways of working, ideas of home and special places and what they meant to the children. Using sketchbooks, the children gathered ideas that later formed the basis of their creative activities back in school. They worked in a range of media, creating drawings, sculptures and paintings and showing the process of their ideas and thinking as well as the products. They made drawings, sculptures and paintings that culminated in an exhibition.

Being treated as artists allows children to explore their own ideas and how these can be developed. They become involved in exploring art practice in conversation with others. Through open discussion about creativity and the notion of being an artist, the children see their work and ideas being taken seriously.

Thorough documentation of the children's thoughts, feelings and ideas is fundamental to the $5 \times 5 \times 5$ approach. Written observations (often by parents), photographs and videos provide the basis for reflection and further planning by the artist and teachers.

Children's questions were focused on the use of materials, the stories about the sculptures, and where ideas come from. Discussion with Edwina was an important part of validating and respecting the children's ideas. The relationship between the adults and the children was central to the process – imaginative, narrative play was valued and discussed. An important part of each workshop was for the children to reflect on their experiences and discuss how they wanted to develop their ideas in different directions. The children benefited from seeing how Edwina generated, reflected upon, refined and realised her own ideas. She took their ideas seriously and also showed them how their ideas informed her own artwork.

Children readily talked about themselves as creative learners and artists:

Jamie (6 years): 'I am going to tell my dad that I have an exhibition and invite him to come to it…'

Jamie was able to find a vehicle for expressing his fascinations in boats and ships; he spent a great amount of time drawing, researching and transforming his smaller drawings into large-scale drawings and models. He developed confidence in his own ideas and was able to share these with other children and with adults. Being treated with respect, as artists, allowed the children to explore their own ideas about how these can be developed without fear of failure. They became involved in exploring art practice in conversation with others, by asking open-ended questions, making meaning, and understanding and developing work in a supportive environment.

CASE STUDIES

Figure 4.1 Ship, Jamie, Age 6, Victoria Art Gallery, Bath

Figure 4.2 Ship, marker pen, by Jamie, Age 6

CASE STUDIES

Figure 4.3 Jamie's story, Age 6

'Being an Artist' workshops provided a context for children to try out new ideas, to practise new skills, to explore relationships and to deepen their understanding - the essential ingredient of children's relationships with materials gives them multiple possibilities of expression. Open access to materials sought to open wide possibilities in terms of where children might take their artwork and find new lines of enquiry.

Working alongside children in the 'Being an Artist' workshops allowed me to see the strategies that helped to support children's concept of themselves as artists. The quality of attention given to the children seems to be key; the design of the space and the range and provision of materials and resources with emphasis on open-ended materials were also important. Children had a chance to choose materials from a range of media and to learn to recognise the affordances and opportunities of different tools and techniques.

Planning creative spaces, inside and out, that are flexible and responsive to children's interests and fascinations, seem to capture their imagination and encourage their lines of enquiry. This suggests that carefully chosen resources that reflect children's interests can provide provocations for creative and critical thinking, alongside meaningful contexts for initiating artwork. I found that valuing Bo's preferences and entitlement to choose their modes of representation by providing a wide range of tools and materials nurtured her creativity. Documentation was also an important element of each session and was used to observe, analyse, interpret and illustrate each child's creative potential.

Parents who are also professional artists or artist educators, as well as those interested in children's art, work alongside the children and may bring artistic skills or creative conversations to the table; but what they do not define are prescriptions for learning or preconceived outcomes. This contrasts with more traditional models of 'school art' that may offer little educational or artistic value if the learning is already predefined by adults (often denigrated to pre-made models or stencils) prescribed by a national curriculum. This development of a shared understanding and dialogue about ideas is vital in a climate of enquiry offering children the opportunity of making a personal connection to experiences and ideas.

Annual evaluations of the workshops show that children like the space they are given to develop their own ideas without being directed or activities prescribed. Children have said: 'We like being able to do what we want to do, and Penny and Jane help us if we need it' ... they 'like the space to think'. Children are offered subtle encouragement to develop their creativity. The adults aim to show appropriate (not lax or overemphasised) recognition and praise, witnessing children's efforts and encouraging each individual to share ideas with the group. 'Being an Artist' explores notions of ownership, relevance, innovation, control and co-participation, where control over process and content is handed back to the learner.

Making a museum, Freshford Primary School

Discarded objects – a beach ball and a rusty tin – found among feathers, pine cones, shells and sticks, fascinating in their incongruity, were picked up and brought back to the classroom. These began interest in collections and were a source of inspiration for fantasies to take root and grow. Fragments of walks – brought back in the form of memories, photographs and sounds. The classroom became a space to share 'treasures', to talk about their meanings and connections, with time to listen, linger, wonder and speculate.

On a wet winter walk, we find 'a stick what looks like antlers' and 'a piece of the moon' (conker shell). Lots and lots of sticks, leaves and grass are secreted in pockets. Many tiny, striped snail shells seem at first to be all the same, but actually 'they are all different and beautiful'. We bring our treasures back and share our thoughts and memories. The objects represent other things, real and imaginary. We recall walks with our families and things we've found before. We find a discarded beach ball: 'I think there's a beach nearby. Maybe it's a secret beach'.

All our special sticks are collected together in the classroom. The children share their ideas with each other about what the sticks can represent: 'sticks are lovely' and they can become 'antlers – a deer's hat', 'a pretend fishing rod', 'rockets' and 'a rainbow'. The children create new things with the sticks: a dreamcatcher, a picture frame, magic wands, swords and boats. Everyone shares information and inspiration while we discuss the endless possibilities of the stick.

Another cold and muddy morning, the children set off to find the 'secret beach'. They have drawn a map [this is a frequent response in 5 × 5 × 5], 'so we know which way to go'. We catch the wind in plastic bags and call down the clouds that can take us to the secret beach. 'The cloud's called Holly and you have to shout for her'. We float leaf boats and a sledge for 'a teeny weeny elf' down a rainwater 'waterfall' in the road. Adding to our collections, we find a rusty tin 'that might be gold or jewels'.

The children and adults bring in their 'special things' from home, objects they have found. We try to guess what some of them are: 'an olden day thing', 'a bit of a fallen-off wooden church'. We all listen carefully to each other's stories. 'We found it on holiday. First my daddy made it for my mummy. She wore the necklace all the time on holiday.' The children enjoy each other's memories, which prompt further recollections. They keep their things in 'special boxes' at home: 'I got a whole collection of this stuff.' Each object has a place on the big shared blue carpet, and we photograph them all.

CASE STUDIES

> The children decide they want to share the story and their memories with others. They could 'turn all the classroom and playground into a museum', but instead they decide to 'make the museum in the wall on the terrace' [a rough country wall of huge stones]. They 'make a hole in the wall and dig it out and put the things inside' and, over three weeks, create a 'Museum of Found Objects' that includes photographs of their special things and objects they make from the sticks and other things they have collected. Their museum is 'the best thing we've had ever,' and the children decide to celebrate it with a grand opening for parents and siblings. It is a way of sharing an ongoing fascination with collections and 'precious stuff,' and its contents connect the children to their families and the world around them.
>
> 'You are seeing the inside of something when you see it with your heart,' says one of the children. 'You find out more and more.'

Figure 4.4 Outdoor Museum, Freshford Primary School

Tommy's book

A pirate theme had evolved from time spent in the Quiet Garden with a group of 4- to 5-year-old Reception year children. The ship that the children built outside developed into a large boat built in the school hall, constructed from chicken wire and plaster of Paris. Tommy said 'The boat is a hundred, thousand years old'; the boys and Tommy in particular were fascinated with maps, treasure and old books. On one occasion in the school hall, I had laid a table with a variety of Scrapstore materials, mark-making options, paper, fabrics and some old postcards from The Historic Palaces collection.

Tommy, whose grandfather had recently died, collected all of the postcards together and began to make another book.

'I'm fascinated in books, in funeral books, my Dad's Dad has died. The cards remind me of my Dad's Dad. I went to my Dad's Mum's house and loads of people came to my Dad's Mum's house. I can't really remember what happened then... I'm

■ ■ ■ ■ CASE STUDIES

> going to save some pictures for my Mum and Dad. (Sticking cards to paper) I'm saving that one, that one, not this one, because it's like a funeral (postcard of cups and saucers.) The cups and saucers remind me, because usually people eat afterwards. Jesus got crucified, I used to say my Grandma got crucified. So, I making a funeral book, this reminds me of the funeral. I'm cutting the paper, it's too big, the pictures won't fit in, I'm not going to draw it… I've got to fold it, so it's a funeral book.'
>
> Tommy searches the table for other materials; he found some shells. 'They might be interesting to put on the front page.' He stuck these down with Sellotape. 'There, I've drawn my face.' He then writes 'author by Tommy'. 'The book and pictures tell me about my Dad's Dad.' He then went to another table and modelled a pirate ship from clay. At the end of the year, all of the children's drawings, constructions and documentation were exhibited at our cultural centre, the Egg for parents and teachers to see.
>
> Tommy's Dad was visibly moved when he saw Tommy's books and the documentation that revealed how his son was making sense of the loss he so deeply felt.

■ **Figure 4.5** Tommy's book, St Stephen's Primary School, Bath

School Without Walls is a co-enquiry, a residency-based model of experiential and creative learning that transforms both the curriculum and the learning culture in schools.

Transposing 'school' to an arts environment prompts both teachers and children to interrogate and reshape teaching and learning. School Without Walls poses the question 'What is school, and how can we do school differently?' For example, *School Without Walls* projects begin by taking up residency with whole classes of children and inserting the creative learning space into a chosen cultural setting in which the

CASE STUDIES

conventions and frameworks associated with the 'classroom' begin to disappear. Children are placed at the centre of their own learning, so that the themes, programmes and content of learning are largely directed by the children, facilitated through a method of co-enquiry. Adults (including artists, educators and mentors) work alongside the children 'as companions in learning' to facilitate meaningful, creative enquiries in real-life contexts. Arts, media and design education – using creative methods and creative pedagogies – includes hands-on learning with new and digital technologies. This process develops a repertoire of 'learning to learn' skills and competencies and has shown increased motivation, purposeful engagement, authentic learning and social empowerment. School Without Walls illustrates how working intensively with the arts in schools, and working directly with artists in cultural settings, promotes creativity as a way of life, offering a deep knowledge of oneself and others, offering meaningful learning and establishing links with the world in a creative way.

Children are engaged in the cultural life of the place where they live as active citizens and stewards of the environment, helping children become confident and progressive thinkers who feel a deep sense of connection and purpose. School Without Walls is doing school differently. The city is a campus for learning. Children are agents of their own learning, as active citizens, co-designing learning alongside adults who trust in children's ideas, their imagination, curiosity and questions – giving them time, space and quality attention. Children are co-researchers and adults are companions in learning. This approach also reduces behaviour problems and improves attendance. They practice habits of mind that artists use, such as curiosity, self-awareness and critical thinking, alongside learning how to make art and talk about it within a group. To perceive, to think, to make judgements and to imagine alternatives: these are all attitudes of mind associated with art practice. Such an intensive creative education experience offers many opportunities for children to explore their relationship with school and their own learning, with their peers, with educators and artists, and with their community. Communication and well-being are important aspects of the School Without Walls residency.

Figure 4.6 Year 4, Batheaston Primary School

■ ■ ■ ■ **CASE STUDIES**

Research question: *'How do we explore "identity" through the power of the arts?'*

Mentor, Liz Elders, 5 × 5 × 5 = creativity / House of Imagination

The class teacher Kate felt this was particularly significant to her class, which all the way through the school had been a disparate and diverse group. The intention was to co-create situations, through working with the artists, where children had to come to appreciate each other's skills, talents, ways of working and dispositions and to build relationships, encourage co-operation and facilitate collaboration.

■ **Figure 4.7** Djordje Ozbolt exhibition, Holburne Museum

The Holburne Museum provided their creative space alongside access to their exhibitions and collections for the children's initial visit. The children could revisit works at any time during the day. They were encouraged to sketch what they were curious about. They were more engaged and sustained this for longer than was anticipated by the teacher. The Holburne's Head of Learning, Christina Parker, was surprised by what they found interesting: a silver spoon, a goblet, a Djordje Ozbolt exhibition and paintings by Thomas Gainsborough. They were invited to respond to and share their interpretations of the artworks through different creative media, including dressing up, drama, clay and drawing/painting materials. The children wanted to imitate the poses and dress up as the people in the paintings.

Back in school, one day per week with the artist, the children's interests in the Ozbolt works led to enquiry into cartoonish styles of drawing and storytelling. The artist introduced layering of images using acetate in order to further the children's interpretation of visual arts through transformation of imagery, and the children continued to imagine the lives of people in the paintings.

CASE STUDIES

The class before the project was considered challenging and difficult to take out on trips. But after the success of the first visit, they returned and used public transport to get to and from the museum, keeping up the connection and sustaining the enquiry.

After a visit to a Pieter Bruegel the Elder exhibition where the children had been fascinated by the different scenes within a large picture, the artist, educator and mentor reflected on how to refocus in on their aims – identity and creating contexts in which they could appreciate each other's talents and learn to collaborate. What could the Bruegel works, of scenes set in landscapes, offer up to them in terms of possibilities? Ideas emerged and the artist proposed to the class the concept of a group painting, small groups each working on a panel, that would connect together as a whole (as in the Hockney study below) to make one large class picture that would represent them as a class.

Figure 4.8 David Hockney study

The panel painting process took 6 weeks. They formed their own groups but were challenged to think about what each person could bring to the group, how they would complement each other, rather than just choose their friends.

They co-designed and co-created ideas and themes to represent themselves and each other, things in their lives, their likes.

The artist and educator facilitated class collaboration, negotiation, conflict & resolution through class meetings at the start and end of each session to decide on each panel and how the 'world' they created could come together as a whole. *Helen was brilliant at holding those conflicts and conversations. How do we resolve and debate those kinds of things with children?*

One example is the coastline: The children had to negotiate how this would look, the colour and shade of the sand, where rocks were placed, how it would connect. This they did largely, but there is one section of coastline that doesn't line up

> *where the argument wasn't resolved. As in life, they had to accept that not all things are resolved.*
>
> There were weekly reflection sessions throughout where they shared observations, reflected, analysed and interpreted before thinking about possibilities that worked with the grain of these. This is an example from the educator–artist reflections at the end of the project:
>
> 'The original ideas dramatically changed as a consensus was reached…it was fascinating as it was a strong conversation, full of strong differing ideas, and took lots of work to find the compromise. These themes of working alongside each other, and difference colliding, collaboration, sharing ideas… stealing ideas…changing ideas, ownership of ideas, honouring each other's ideas continued throughout the life of the painting … They maintained wonderful focus throughout the weeks of the sketching and painting process and learnt so much as each panel was worked on in small groups, and brought together as a whole, connecting to other groups during the process.'
>
> In the evaluation process at the end of the project, these were the key areas of learning that they identified:
>
> - **Positive professional relationships.** The educator felt that the ongoing dialogue between educator, artist, mentor and cultural centre staff had helped her to look deeper into what the children were doing and thinking.
> - **Support and challenge for vulnerable learners.** A significant area of vulnerability for these children was their ability to sustain positive social skills, relations and dispositions. The artist and educator co-crated powerful and challenging learning contexts for the vulnerable learners and across the whole class.
> - **Immersion in high-quality art.** The relationship with the Holburne Museum immersed the children in high-quality art from Bruegel and Gainsborough to contemporary artists like Ozbolt. The Holburne offered the children a greater sense of freedom, space, time and calmness to get lost in their own learning.
> - **The power of the arts.** The arts provided a way of learning, a way to explore differences of identity, interests, dispositions and ideas, and ways of engaging with each other and collaborating. It provided 100 languages in which to explore, think and express their ideas.

AUTHENTIC LEARNING IN REAL-WORLD CONTEXTS

Supporting children and young people to be engaged in meaningful creative enquiries as protagonists of their own learning, in real-world contexts, in ways that aim to engage their heads, hands and hearts. While we do not collude with the performance-led agenda, all schools have witnessed improved SATs (Standard Assessment Tasks) and Ofsted (Office for Standards in Education, Children's Services and Skills) reports. This approach also has implications for ITE (initial teacher education) and CPD (continuing professional development) – embedding creativity and critical thinking in the curriculum.

CASE STUDIES

CO-ENQUIRY AND INTRINSIC MOTIVATION

Children are collaborators, not consumers, and participation is key. School Without Walls has developed a rigorous and well-documented practice that helps to nurture children as active citizens, helping to shape their own cultural lives. Creative co-enquiry is the pedagogical approach that is developed through collaboration between artists and educators. A creative provocation or question is devised by the artist and teaching team, one that they believe will resonate with the children and provide a catalyst for learning. The teacher and artist carefully notice the children's responses using observations in the moment, journaling to develop a questioning mindset with the children, and staff reflection meetings to understand the children's interests and the connections being made in the learning. Lastly, the artist supports the teacher to devise the next creative opportunity that, crucially, will help the children persist in their enquiries and take their learning deeper. As the process repeats, the adults in the room are carefully scaffolding creative learning, not driven by outcome but led by the children.

Gallery of Learning

School Without Walls has developed a creative pedagogy in which students are agents of their own education, their making and thinking. Children develop artful thinking during this process. The skills of the artist are brought to bear in providing novel, open learning opportunities, helping children develop new skills through their creative endeavours. However, above all, the artist brings their own artistic habits of mind into the room. School Without Walls is a moment of profound enquiry, of action research. The artist is modelling a questioning mindset and exploring ideas creatively. The teacher is stepping back from learning outcomes to focus almost entirely on the children. The children are being challenged to explore their own ideas. There are no wrong answers. The goals are well-being, engagement and developing a respectful learning collaboration. Three areas were identified for evaluation through consultation with the School Without Walls team, led by Headteachers, and informed by their School Development Plans:

- evidence of positive and measurable impact on well-being and engagement across the course of the project
- performance progress in the school's chosen focus areas: oracy and learning resilience for all children and specific learning benefits for vulnerable children
- improvements in teachers' practice

MY STOMACH – GENEVE

'My starting point is when we had our first lesson with Catherine and she asked us to close our eyes (like she always does!). Then she told us to imagine a journey through our body and we could use any kind of transport to use on our travel. A clear, vivid image appeared and it was my stomach! It was not a scientific image, but my own that was a lovely picture – better than the look of a real one. On my mind the small,

CASE STUDIES

medium and giant bubble pops depending on size. If it was small, it popped one second before it was made, medium can live like a normal bubble! Finally, the big one lasts as long as two of them put together and more.

First, I used an orange, soft pastel to make big circles (bubble) some overlapped each other! Then I used a red-coloured soft pastel to make a slightly small bubble inside the bigger one. After all of the bubble making stomach I made I smudged the outside and then traced to add effects. I thought I was finished and then I made a small bubble and some popped to show a few (in) movement – how many tiny bubbles have been popped? What do you think it looked like when you first saw it? Why did you think of that?

After I finished I felt proud and have to admit it looked just like I've seen in my mind or even better! Even though some of my work turns out to something different, but luckily it turned (out) just as I imagined in my mind. Every time I looked at it – (it) reminds me of my fascinating journey through my stomach. How I loved and gave my heart on this piece to show that I cared and took my very time to finish this. If I never gave such love it may not be here for you to see.'

Figure 4.9 Geneve, Age 10, St Michael's Junior School, Bath

St Andrew's Primary School at Bath School of Art and Design
Fine Art | making placards with Anna Gravelle and Penny Hay

We met under the tree in the grounds. We invited the Year 3 children what a world without art would look like and from that they devised slogans that were used to make protest placards using cut tape.

CASE STUDIES

Figure 4.10 Art Placards, St Andrew's Primary School, Bath at the School of Art and Design, Bath Spa University

Activity: Creating slogans and placards to protest the cuts within arts education
Suzanne: A slogan is like a logo with words.
Maisie: Be positive and your dreams will come true.
Danny: Earth is drawing, drawing is Earth. Save art, save nature.
Cormac: Art is everywhere.
Jakub: Art is using your imagination.
Luke V.T.: Art is being creative.
Maisie: If you make a mistake, try again.
Nina: Art is life.
Isaac: No art, no imagination.
Maurya: Save art, save creativity.

The final installation was a creative manifesto:

Art is in everything
Art is lol
I enjoy art
I heart creativity
Art grows every where
Amazing art
No art no imagination
Positive art positive life
Art is everything, no art:-(
You can make art
Art is love
Art is life
I want to keep art
Art is amazing
No art, no world

■ ■ ■ ■ **CASE STUDIES**

St Andrews CE Primary School with Bath School of Art and Design

Bath Spa University | Case study written by Liz Elders, Mentor 5 × 5 × 5 = creativity

This event was the culmination of the children's experience of School Without Walls at Bath School of Art and Design, where they had spent 4 days in residence during the Graduate Degree Show. The children worked alongside lecturers, students and the 5 × 5 × 5 = creativity team, exploring processes involved in art and design and creative and critical thinking. A particular theme was around failure, failing well and perseverance through problems. The children were invited to share their learning at the 5 × 5 × 5 = creativity annual conference: Creative Revolution with Sir Ken Robinson.

At the beginning of the morning, everyone assembles in the foyer of Commons in front of the gigantic media wall whilst students and staff of the University go about their daily endeavours unaware of what is about to unfold. Penny Hay invited the children to think about their experience of School Without Walls over the last few days at the School of Art and Design at the Sion Hill Campus: 'If you had to tell your friend one thing about your experience, what would it be'? Sam, their teacher suggests: 'When we have these ideas, ask yourself why? Develop your idea.'

Anthony Head sets the scene for the morning: 'Who likes computer games, toys and mechanical physics?'

'What's mechanical physics' (one of the children ask)?

Anthony shows them a marble run toy that he has brought along for them to play with during the morning. 'Part of mechanical physics is about how things move, fall, collide – gravity.'

He shows them the media wall towering two stories high above them. 'It's like 30 TV screens joined together with a computer behind it.' Anthony shows them the computer desktop displayed across the media wall screens. 'Guess how high?' Children call out: *1500 metres, 8 metres* … 'Stop there, it's actually 7.5 metres so you were really close.'

'We're going to make a marble run on the screen. You're going to redesign it.'
'Marvellous Marbles,' they read off the dialogue box.
It looks like 'Little Big Planet'.
Marbles run down the wall:
There's more coming.
That one just disappeared.

Anthony: 'You're seeing a basic view of what it might be. We're going to divide the screen into 5 sections. Each group will design one section.' [The sections will then be re-programmed by Anthony using the children's designs.] 'It can have ramps, pivots, seesaws. Agree a theme for your section. Do a background picture. One person draw and design the ramps etc. Someone design some characters and what it can do [animate it]. The circles are spinny things and you can design pictures that will spin around. Some of the platforms are slippery/icy, some are bouncy. You can hear the sound of the screen too – sounds for the platforms and see-saw.'

Max: *I've got an idea: So they go down the ramp, it's kind of sticky.*
Matthew: *But how does it make it move?*

CASE STUDIES

Jon explains, draws it.

Max: *I wonder what they do – the bits that look like screws?*
Matthew: *I think when something lands on it, it does something.*
Jon: 'This one might do something'. [They all observe the media wall – to understand more of the mechanics.]

Max talks with Vicky, who is doing the background. Max explains: *Space 1, it's not a living thing, Space 1 is like a dust cloud that sucks it in.*

Matthew: *Make it look like a tornado.*
Max: *Make it look not real-like.*

Max returns his attention to designing the 'stripy' ramps and balls to look like *a little bouncy planet*.
They check in on who is doing each role in the group:

Max: *I'm doing the actual thing. It's better if you do the background 'or' the characters. Better if you do 1 thing. Which would you like to do?*
Vicky: *The background. I need to do the aliens.* [Thinking out loud to me.] *I'm not sure why I'm doing characters? I'm doing the queen.*

I reassure her: 'The characters you're drawing are part of the scene and help us to understand that it's Space.'
Olivia is doing the animated characters that are part of the marble run itself: *Who's doing characters apart from me?*
Matthew and Max have been working together on the design of the run. Matthew checks in with student Jon: '*Is this too technical? Is it better if we …*'

Max: *Shall I try again? I've got a better idea. It could be like this thing where … it could be …*
Jon: 'It has to be a ramp or see-saw, I don't think it can be a tube. … You could have a thing like that that bounces.'
Matthew: *Is this too technical? Can it roll down and the alien goes on it?*
Max: *I know, there could be a UFO on it* [the spinner], *so when the ball lands on it the UFO spins.*

Anthony has explained that as they are working on the design within a short time frame he has designed the programme within certain parameters. He is open to their designs and ideas, but it has to be do-able in the time. Max and Matthew appear to have different and complementary approaches. Max is full of ideas and Matthew is more pragmatic, project-managing in collaboration with Max and design student Jon to focus on the best ideas that they can accomplish within the project brief – much as in professional work situations. It is striking how the children, students and professionals are collaborating as part of one creative design team, all working alongside each other, exchanging ideas, negotiating, making decisions, and taking on specific roles within the team.

Logan: *That could be icy, so that it goes along there and that could be bouncy.*
Arsia: *This could be bouncy, so it bounces on the ice and then this wobbles.*
Sennan: *It's the street, it's all dark and moody.*
Arsia: *This one might breathe fire* [the dragon character to be animated].
Logan: *This character is pretty cool. Do you know Street Fighter* [to the student]? *I made it like that.*
Arsia: *How can my dragon breath fire on the building?*

All the children in the group have a very definite colour scheme (black, red and gold) and resist any suggestions/questions from the adults about adding more colour.

The children and adults get a look at the first phase that has been programmed on the media wall [the marble run, without backgrounds and characters].

That's my shot!
That see-saw needs to go up there, the ball gets stuck.

Anthony explains that this is how designers work: 'We design it, test it and then redesign it.'

Does the shark [character] *ever change? Do we need to change it?*

Anthony: 'Is there a bit that's not being used that we need to change?'

It's going to work I think ... it's the see-saw.
No, the spinny thing!

Anthony: 'One way is to make it go faster <u>or</u> we could make the see-saw shorter so it goes down?'
Sam: 'Look at your section. Make sure you have everything that is needed. What needs doing (e.g., decorating a platform)? Make sure everyone knows what you have to finish in your group.'
Max: *Matthew that's really good. Yes, put spiky bits along there.*
Matthew: *The problem was it didn't spin.*

Olivia, with support from Max, has written a numbered list of what needs doing and is checking the list, ticking things off as they are completed.

Olivia and Max explain the changes they want to make to the design to turn the platform into a snake and revise the angle of the platform. Jon encourages them to liaise with Anthony.

Matthew to one of the Under Sea group about the shark character: *Does it really say Hi?* 'Can they get to the shark?'

'Yes, it can.' 'I don't want to see it on the computer screen, I'm going to wait to see it on the big screen [media wall].'

Children cluster around the computer and Logan confidently explains what they are doing to Sir Ken Robinson, who gives them positive feedback, asserting their identity as artists.

CASE STUDIES

Figure 4.11 Sir Ken Robinson responding to the children's artwork on the Media Wall, Bath Spa University

Batheaston Primary School

'How do we explore 'identity' through the power of the arts?'

The focus of this project was around identity and the celebration of diversity. This was recognised by Kate (class teacher) as of particular importance for her Year 4 class. Her aim at the beginning was to co-create situations, through working with the artists, where children had to come to appreciate each other's skills, talents, ways of working and dispositions. Eleven full- or half-day sessions were co-delivered by the artists and educators between February and June. Framed by the initial question, the focus of the artist-led sessions was on exploring ways in which the arts could be used as a vehicle to bring children together within their learning, encouraging co-operation and the appreciation of identity and diversity within the class.

The relationship with the cultural partner, The Holburne Museum, and with Christina as Head of Learning, was key. The class, along with artists and educators, explored the permanent museum collection on display and also viewed two temporary exhibitions of paintings: the work of Djordje Ozbolt and *Bruegel: Defining a Dynasty*. These visits acted as creative provocations for their own ideas and later creative work. Children were encouraged to respond to the artworks in different ways, using their journals to sketch, draw and paint, writing notes and reflections about their experiences, and modelling their responses in clay.

Adults also observed children's spontaneous reactions to the artworks, physically mimicking the poses of characters in the portraits they encountered, using their whole bodies for expression. Drawing on this physical exploration, the children were invited to

■ ■ ■ ■ **CASE STUDIES**

further explore and share their interpretations of the artworks through different creative media, including dressing up, role-play, drama and sculpting in clay. They were encouraged to imagine the stories that the artworks would tell, the artists and educators inviting them to make their own interpretations, giving permission to alter the artworks and make them into their own.

Inspired in particular by the work of Bruegel and responding to the initial focus of the enquiry, Helen (artist) worked with the class to produce a collaborative painting of scenes set in landscapes, working in small groups to each produce a part of the canvas. The groups worked through different stages of design and creation, from sketching out their ideas, introducing colour, painting their final panels and bringing them together in the realization of their collective artwork. Their style of painting seemed to be influenced by Ozbolt. In selecting their working groups, children were challenged to think about the skills that different people would bring to the task.

■ **Figure 4.12** Designing the canvas, Year 4, Batheaston Primary School

'A lot of negotiation had to go on. How would they bring these individual pieces together into one whole? For example, a coastline connected several scenes. They had to negotiate how the coastline would look, the colour and shade of the sand, where rocks were placed, how it would connect. There is one section of coastline that doesn't line up between 2 panels where the argument wasn't resolved. One of the children was adamant that he'd planned the shoreline that way and he wasn't going to compromise. Helen was brilliant at holding those conflicts and conversations. How do we resolve and debate those kinds of things with children? Sometimes we are able to resolve issues and find solutions or compromises, but as in life, not all things are resolved.' – Liz, mentor

'School Without Walls was different to any other art I could have imagined. It kind of made us express our art in our way. Crazy, normal, imaginative – all of these things!'

CASE STUDIES

> 'It has meant to me that if everybody works together it could create and amazing piece of work. It has made my learning much more fun and it gives me something to look forward to. I have also experienced much more art work.'
>
> 'School Without Walls is a great way to expand children's minds. I found that I could let my imagination run wild! Everybody had an idea that was used. School Without Walls has helped me understand more about art and had made it more fun. I'd like it to happen again!'
>
> 'I would like to use this in my future work with team members in the classroom. There are many talented people that I work with and think it would be a great opportunity to give them more time to reflect on the children and to consider where our learning should go. Furthermore, this could be the same after an activity that the class have worked on. Which conversations were heard and how we can reflect on this as a team?'
>
> 'They learnt a great deal from working alongside Helen and Christina (Holburne) and wanted to know more! They were particularly excited about seeing the Gainsborough Paintings in place at the Holburne and being able to learn about the techniques used. This was far more relevant and exciting than learning about the painting in the classroom with me.'

IMMERSION IN HIGH-QUALITY ART

The relationship with the Holburne Museum offered many opportunities for the children to experience high-quality art as a provocation for their learning. Kate reflected that she had been surprised by the reactions of many of her children and the ways in which they had responded to the artworks and the space of the Holburne.

'Going to the Holburne there were children who really surprised me, there were children who were far more engaged. Wandering round the gallery I thought this could be tricky, they haven't got the best attention spans. We set them a fairly simple challenge on the first session, to wander round and find something that would really interest them, to sketch it and bring it back. Like with other things, when you try to plan your day you think, how much time do we give them for that? They could have just stayed there all day…there were several boys who were so engrossed and really engaged and just in their own zone. They weren't worried about what anyone else was doing, they just wanted to be in their zone sketching, they were fab in the Holburne.'

'HOUSE OF IMAGINATION' (YEAR 2)

Imagination is seeing things that are not there.

– Suzanne

Artist Helen Lawrence created a museum of tiny objects. What stories could these objects tell? What imagined world might they belong to? The children created small worlds through playing with the objects, imagining, drawing and telling their stories.

In response to No. 1's doll house exhibition and inspired by the Brambly Hedge books, the children created rooms for their small creatures. *'We made the mouse homes using extra heart. This means when you love something and really care about it. We want the mice to be happy, that's why we have lights, so they are not scared of the dark.'* – Lily

Jakub positioned his house high up in the tree *'with its friends – it has feathers'.* He faced his drawing outwards *'because that's the outside of the world'.*

Figure 4.13 Small Worlds, Year 2, St Andrew's Primary School, Bath

'SOUNDS OF HOUSE' (YEAR 3)

We were inspired by the parts of our houses that can't be seen. The children focused on the mysteries and answers that come from listening. We explored how sound can be both descriptive and ambiguous. Through 2 workshops sessions we learned more about sound, including 100 different things that can be heard in a silent classroom if we listen carefully, and that music can inspire stories and create imaginative drawings. We shared memories from our home-life and we found ways of telling them without words or pictures but with the making of sound.

– Jono Burgess, artist

The children agreed that *'sound is better' 'if you see the picture, it gives it away,'* suggesting that sounds leave more room for imagination and interpretation.

The children have shared their own 'Sounds of House' in this exhibition. Please put on the headphones – what can you hear, what story do you imagine?

CASE STUDIES ▪ ▪ ▪ ▪

▪ **Figure 4.14** Sounds of House, Year 3 children at St Andrew's School, Bath

▪ **Forest of Imagination** is a unique collaboration between the creative and cultural industries and the community of Bath. Forest of Imagination, co-founded by Grant Associates and House of Imagination (formerly 5 × 5 × 5=creativity), has grown out of partnership and collective ambition to make a difference in the city. We want to create spaces that inspire and feed the creativity of our children. Forest of Imagination deliberately brings the inspirational experience and sensations of nature and wildness to our doorsteps – it is about the creative ecology of the city, with collaboration across generations and between industries. Creative installations in the heart of the city and in nature address bigger themes about the environment and climate change, sharing ideas through our collective imagination.

We need to develop habits of mind for life-wide and life-long creativity, developing creative ideas into action, and connect children's learning to opportunities to make a better world. Forest of Imagination reveals the collaborative and creative ecology of the city in a new and engaging way and gives permission for a new way of experiencing and enjoying nature in a city environment. Over seven years, Forest of Imagination has demonstrated both social and civic innovation – unlocking the creative capacity of a community and expressing this through the joyful transformation of a familiar landscape or public place, all within a strong ecological and sustainable framework. Designers and artists working with children and young people are at the heart of this project and are demonstrating their capacity to lead, inspire and inform change through creative design and collaborative working.

▪ **Forest of Imagination** shines a light on the importance of global forests, the capacity of Bath as a creative ecosystem, the natural wonder of the city and above all the capacity of Forests to inspire creativity in everyone. Forest of Imagination is about creative place making through temporary transformation of familiar city spaces and creative social engagement. It emphasises how everyone can engage in a conversation about imagination and creativity set within an urban landscape and public realm context.

■ ■ ■ ■ **CASE STUDIES**

A CREATIVE LEARNING INVITATION FOR CHILDREN AND TEACHERS

Aims

To work in collaboration with educators, schools and children to research children and young people's responses to nature, their local environment and the global environmental crisis and ecological emergency

To promote the health and well-being of children and teachers, through connectedness to nature and the arts.

To work with diverse communities across the city and surrounding area, through the schools and a focus on their local environment (lived-in and green spaces).

To work with everyone's unique capacities: 'Imagination is a unique human capacity'.

To engage educators, children and schools in co-enquiry, co-research and co-construction and the notion of tinkering, invention and being playful.

To promote learning through the arts and artistic excellence in creative education.

Pedagogical principles and approach

The invitations were designed in conjunction with House and Forest of Imagination using the principles and approach researched over many years with schools, teachers, children, artists and art organisations. Key principles included the following: a belief in children's potential, listening to and trusting in children's ideas; a process of co-enquiry and dialogue; educators as co-protagonists alongside children; enquiry and expression through many forms of communication such as dance, drama, art, music, technology and writing; and engagement with creative professionals.

■ **Figure 4.15** Perry Harris artwork for Forest of Imagination

CASE STUDIES

Being in nature: This co-enquiry was based upon the children's exploration and responses to nature or green space and the sense of well-being that it evokes. Children were able to explore their feelings, thoughts, imaginings and wonderings about being in nature by being playful with words, sounds, movement and music, creating soundscapes, dance and film.

Figure 4.16 Clare Day, Clay Forest

Landscape city outlook: Using viewing platforms to look out onto the local environment and city, children imagined what they would want the city to be like in 'their' future? Drawing upon this perspective, small groups were invited to co-design a 3D vision of their landscape city or renewed local environment through the process of making with paper, card or clay.

Figure 4.17 Jess Palmer, Urban Forest

Forest City: Exploring the local lived environment, green spaces or riverside in relation to climate change. Sharing their perspective on issues of climate change and how they want their lived environment to be? Creating narratives in poetry, prose or spoken word linked to the idea of the 'memory of the water', 'following a river and listening to its voice', 'river running through', and the 'many stories of the place' or imagining their story in the future where the city has been greened or rewilded. Children imagined their story in the future where the city has been greened or rewilded, to design and make a Forest City using found natural materials and reusable and recycled materials.

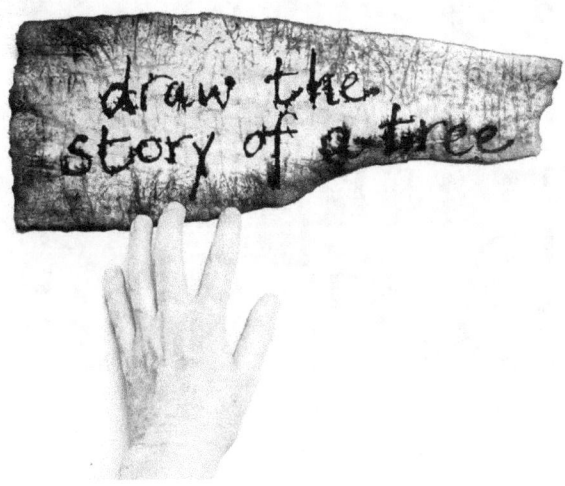

Figure 4.18 Clare Day, Gift to the Forest

Tales of a Forest of Imagination: Engaging children in tinkering with words and images to create a Tree or Forest of Imagination. A process using collected images, words, reworked artworks to be playful with, in a process of story-making. Creating illustrated books to form a Tree of Books or Forest of Imagination.

A River Running Through: A co-enquiry based upon the theme of the river running through the surrounding area. It relates to local history, local springs, health and well-being. It explores water as a basic human need, sustainability, and the global environmental crisis and draws upon the idea of the water that connects us all. The enquiry can be explored and expressed through the visual arts, including journaling, photography, drawing, painting and clay.

Trees of Hope: A co-enquiry based upon artistic reconnections with nature and the land linked to the Trees of Hope project in collaboration with WOMAD (World of Music, Arts & Dance), an eco-educational project with images, people, land, music and dance of Zimbabwe.

Edible Forest: This was a longer-term project for a class involving them in designing and making a small-scale, sustainable, edible forest or landscape for the school grounds. The project also involved families. It engaged the children in discussion about the global and environmental crisis; positive actions for the environment;

and personal health and well-being. The enquiry process involved dialogue, design, engineering, project management, growing food, and creative cookery.

Figure 4.19 Helen Lawrence, Edible Forest

Activity: With colleagues, collect a series of 'highlights' or glow moments (MacLure 2010) from your children to co-design a whole school exhibition. Invite parents in for a discussion about the value of art in children's development.

REFERENCES AND FURTHER READING

Laevers, F. (2015) *Making Care and Education More Effective Through Wellbeing and Involvement: An Introduction to Experiential Education*. Research Centre for Experiential Education, University of Leuven Belgium.

MacLure, M. (2010) The Offence of Theory. *Journal of Education Policy*, 25 (2), 277–286.

SUGGESTED WEBSITES

http://houseofimagination.org/
http://www.forestofimagination.org.uk/
http://www.schoolwithoutwalls.org.uk/]

CHAPTER 5
THE ROLE OF THE ADULT

Figure 5.1 Adults as companions in children's learning

This chapter will explore the adult–child relationship and particularly examine the focus on the role of the adult in supporting children's creative development and identity as artists. We aim to offer a model of practice for how adults can support children's creative development and identity as artists and how children engage with adults as role models. The chapter will outline the characteristics of creative teaching and learning and show how these can be applied and extended to teaching and learning in art and design. This includes adults who

- are willing to observe, listen to and work closely with children's ideas with endless curiosity
- understand what it means to be creative and interested in how children learn and who model the creative process alongside children

THE ROLE OF THE ADULT

- are active learners and model learning for others, and enjoy learning with others, as co-learners, co-constructing knowledge
- work towards transforming themselves and others through learning together.
- show an openness to possibility; talk openly about learning; maintain a readiness to change their points of view; and use conversations, dialogues and rich discourses on learning to arrive at shared understandings
- offer multi-sensory, multi-dimensional learning approaches with vital, rich and creative learning opportunities
- create an ethos of respect for ideas and give time, space and attention to individual learning

THE TEACHER'S ROLE IN FACILITATING ART AND DESIGN ACTIVITIES

The role of the teacher is vital in providing quality learning experiences for children. The following criteria summarise the multifaceted role of the teacher and offer a checklist for review:

- understanding children's stages of development
- planning for progression and differentiation
- organising and managing the learning environment: time, space, resources and people
- encouraging children to take increasing responsibility for their working space
- providing a range of good-quality materials and resources
- observing and interacting with sensitivity
- using and developing language
- providing opportunities for evaluation and reflection
- providing a balance between
    - integrated and discrete activities
    - teacher-structured and child-initiated work
    - individual, group and whole class activities
    - 2D and 3D work
    - small-scale and large-scale work
    - activities based on art, craft and design
    - a range of cultural resources
- assessing and recording
- displaying process as well as product

One of the most important aspects of this role is the quality of interaction between teacher and child. The dialogue that a teacher uses can play a significant part in children's attitudes to their own and others' work. If a child feels supported and is working in an environment that values individual responses, the child will grow in confidence and self-esteem. Children do not respond to lax approval but need to have clear expectations and objectives for their work. The sensitivity of the teacher is crucial in supporting and extending the children's learning. Careful and appropriate questioning can help children focus on the development of their work. Opportunities

THE ROLE OF THE ADULT

need to be provided for child–child and teacher–child interaction as well as whole class sharing and discussion.

Creating a positive learning environment using a variety of strategies

- planning and structuring work that encourages individual responses
- sharing teaching and learning objectives with children
- negotiating activities with children
- organising materials and resources
- presenting and communicating ideas clearly
- working from direct experience
- allowing time for exploration and experimentation
- sharing skills and techniques
- valuing children's ideas and personal responses
- asking open-ended questions
- encouraging discussion with and between children
- valuing process as well as product
- mounting displays as both stimulus for and celebration of the work
- providing opportunities for children to evaluate their own and others' work

Figure 5.2 Adults using sketchbooks alongside children

QUESTIONS TO FOCUS TEACHING AND LEARNING

Will you invite children to work as a whole class, in a group or individually?
What type of questions will you ask to encourage thinking through making?
How will you support children to be experimental and creative?

THE ROLE OF THE ADULT

What opportunities are there for the children to take responsibility for their own learning?
How are the children's personal experiences drawn upon as subject matter?
How will the learning enhance qualities such as independence or self-esteem?
Is the work differentiated in any way?
What opportunities are given for discussion and evaluation?
What does children's work reveal about the way they feel and think?

THE ROLE OF THE ADULT AS A COMPANION IN LEARNING

The notion of the adult as a companion in learning is set in contrast to a teacher-led model of learning. In the Reggio Emilia approach, the 'atelierista' is a 'studio worker, an artisan, a lender of tools, a partner in a quest or journey' (Edwards *et al.* 1998). In *House of Imagination* (formerly $5 \times 5 \times 5 = creativity$), each artist maintains his or her own professional creative practice as a vital component in the research. *House of Imagination* shows how artists can function as 'co-learners' by integrating their own artistic practice with pedagogy, so that artists engage with participants primarily through discussion and exchanging ideas and experiences where shared knowledge is generated.

In *House of Imagination*, the artist works alongside the educators, following the ideas of the children, led by their explorations and their thinking. The process, rather than the end product, is the main focus; 'we are researching the children researching the world'. Children are given the opportunity to explore their own themes and questions and are encouraged to create their own lines of enquiry. Adults' support for children in creative endeavours involves becoming involved in the thinking process; showing respect and genuine interest; using questioning and discourse; being alongside the child; and observing and documenting children's learning.

The pedagogical practices included provocation, the 'self' as a teaching resource, use of the body, the use of professional norms, managing behaviour differently, the use of routine, flexibility of pacing, and the use of open-ended challenge and permission to play. Adults are able to support children in developing art practice (in conversation with others), asking good questions, making sense of experience, and making meaning, so that children can understand and develop work in a supportive environment.

Providing the time and space for children to engage with the processes of being an artist, so that making, thinking, playing and research infuse the pedagogical practice in a holistic way. A number of distinct but interlinked core features of learners' and teachers' engagement can be valued and fostered in each setting: posing questions, play, immersion, innovation, being imaginative, self-determination and risk-taking.

Teaching art creatively includes the use of space and time, fostering self-esteem, offering learners support in creative approaches, involving children in creative thinking skills, encouraging the expression of ideas through a wide variety of expressive media, and encouraging the integration of subject areas through topics holding meaning and relevance to the children's lives.

Children show many motivations for making art for different purposes and in different contexts. Art has been a means of self-expression and has also allowed them to explore ideas and feelings in different modalities. Children are researchers of the world, exploring creative ideas. As adults, we are modelling creative dispositions with children as well as developing enabling contexts in which the children can develop their own interests and express ideas.

Crucially, teachers should prioritise a creative pedagogy rather than a 'default pedagogy' which can be in response to a standards agenda that defines excellence in terms of progress against a limited set of measurable outcomes.

Engaging with children in an authentic way, primarily through discussion and the exchange of ideas and experiences, invites co-constructed, collaborative learning, whereby shared knowledge is generated between adults and children, both as learners. The teacher is a co-learner rather than an infallible expert transmitting knowledge to the participants.

Engaging in a dialogue that explores the creative process helps children to understand their own creativity and imagination.

Here are some prompts that you might use:

What is the imagination?
Where do your ideas come from?
How can you show your creativity?
How do you want to record and share your ideas?
How can you persevere if you make a mistake?

OPPORTUNITIES FOR REFLECTION

What processes and media did you explore?
How did you develop your ideas?
How did looking at artists' work help develop your thoughts and ideas?
How did you share your ideas and processes with others?
How can you share your understanding of creative processes?
How could art be used to develop ideas about personal, social and cultural identity?

THE ROLE OF THE TEACHER

We can use our own creative knowledge and skills to facilitate and enable others' creativity. These processes might include experiential learning, open-ended questioning, a non-judgemental approach, empathy, active listening, reflection, and sharing insights and ideas together.

Children are active makers of meaning rather than passive recipients of knowledge and therefore the role of the teacher is crucial in enabling learners to use art-making as a means to articulate their thoughts and ideas. This involves giving children the opportunity to experiment within a supportive and creative environment. Sharing their own creative skills and dispositions, teachers can inspire children's own interests and creative habits of mind. Careful observation and documentation of children's learning highlight the creative dispositions of being an artist and how these may be supported through creative enquiry. This process requires a culture of open discussion about creative processes and the notion of being an artist.

THE ROLE OF THE ADULT ■ ■ ■ ■

■ **Figure 5.3** Teachers and children documenting learning, St Saviours Infant School, Bath

TEACHER DEVELOPMENT

Our own development as teachers also involves the following aspects:

Developing visual literacy: ways of looking at and talking about art
Developing imaginative responses to a stimulus: possibilities not prescriptions
Exploring and experimenting with materials and processes: using sketchbooks
Giving form to ideas, constructing meaning and developing personal responses
Implications for children's development in art and design
Developing a creative pedagogy

WORKING WITH ARTISTS

Working with artists is an important part of a child's experience of art and design

- as role models, demonstrate creative dispositions, curiosity and openness to possibilities
- as creative enablers, support the expression and communication of ideas in diverse modes
- 'follow the smoke' of developing themes and ideas
- provide creative interventions and provocations for thought and representation

■ ■ ■ ■ **THE ROLE OF THE ADULT**

RESOURCES TO SUPPORT LEARNING IN ART AND DESIGN

Primary Resource Material

People

Teachers
Children
Parents/guardians
Community groups
Local artists, craftspeople, designers, architects…

Objects

Natural objects (e.g., plants, animals, stones, shells, bark and seed pods)
Made objects (e.g., wheels, cogs, kitchen utensils, clothes, musical instruments, toys, containers and textiles)

Children need to be encouraged to collect their own resources and have the opportunity to use these in the development of their ideas.

Places

Galleries
Museums
Parks
Townscapes
Landscapes
Seascapes
Shops
Fairs
Farms…

Secondary Resource Material

Books
Photographs
Prints
Postcards
Slides
Films
Loan services and study collections

It is important to ensure that the needs and interests of **all** children are reflected in the resources shown and used.

THE ROLE OF THE ADULT

EQUAL OPPORTUNITIES

When considering the ways in which we seek to teach in and through art, we should check that what we are teaching takes account of the full and inclusive nature of the subject. We are fortunate in that art can be seen as a universal human activity and, as such, evidence of cultural diversity can be positively celebrated within it. The practice of art crosses boundaries of gender, race and ethnicity. Efforts should be made in practical ways to encourage children to respond to each other in ways which foster genuine cross-cultural understanding, whatever their circumstances and backgrounds.

Developing a leadership role

The 'official' term for this position has varied from specialist to consultant, post-holder, curriculum coordinator, curriculum leader, subject manager and subject leader. Each term brings with it different emphases for the role.

'being engaged in knowing, supporting, monitoring and improving.'

coordinator	adviser	mediator	confidant
supporter	mentor	motivator	advocate
listener	consultant	critical friend	expert
monitor	evaluator	leader	manager
technician	educator	facilitator	initiator

KEY AREAS OF SUBJECT LEADERSHIP

To summarise, the main areas are **policy, learning, people and resources.**

Strategic direction and development of the subject
Within the context of the school's aims and policies, subject leaders develop and implement subject policies, plans, targets and practices.

Teaching and learning
Subject leaders secure and sustain effective teaching of the subject, evaluate the quality of teaching and standards of pupils' achievements and set targets for improvement.

Leading and managing staff
To all those involved in the teaching or support of the subject, subject leaders provide the support, challenge, information and development necessary to sustain motivation and secure improvement in teaching.

Efficient and effective deployment of staff and resources
Subject leaders identify appropriate resources for the subject and ensure that they are used efficiently, effectively and safely.

■ ■ ■ ■ **THE ROLE OF THE ADULT**

> **Questions for the subject leader**
>
> Do you have a clear job description?
> Do you have a professional development programme built in to your contract, based on school priorities?
> Is your role reviewed regularly?
> Are you responsible for the budget?
> Are you able to run professional development sessions and meetings supported by the head?
> Do you have an opportunity for self-evaluative sessions in which teachers share their concerns with you?
> Do you have any non-contact time to address specific issues agreed by the whole staff?
> Do you have an opportunity to carry out classroom-based observations?

ROLES AND RESPONSIBILITIES

The overall purpose of the subject leader is to contribute to school improvement and increase standards through the provision of high-quality teaching and the best possible learning opportunities for children.
   Exemplifying practice by

- working alongside colleagues in their classrooms
- providing or professional development or both
- keeping informed about new initiatives in art and design
- developing an in-depth knowledge of the subject
- providing appropriate resources
- ensuring equal access and opportunity for all children
- planning for and assessing individual achievement
- planning for continuity and progression and evaluating curriculum development
- using effective assessment procedures and record-keeping systems
- monitoring and evaluating progress and achievement
- liaising with parents, governors and the community

> **Activity**
>
> **Checklist: how can I improve my effectiveness?**
>
> Do you ...
> > have good working relationships with colleagues?
> > work alongside teachers in the classroom?
> > keep up to date with new ideas?
> > attend professional development courses and provide feedback to staff?
> > encourage staff to attend courses?
> > liaise with head and colleagues on policy development and review?

THE ROLE OF THE ADULT

- plan and interpret meaningful schemes of work with colleagues?
- oversee the assessment and recording of children's progress?
- determine resources needed?
- liaise with outside agencies?
- organise and lead professional development sessions at school for staff?
- provide support and advice to colleagues?
- monitor and evaluate progress?
- provide support for children with special educational needs?
- maintain an overview of long term development?

Evidence of success

Have you had an influence on school development planning and the status of art and design?
Have you had an influence on the continuity and progression in art and design?
Have you had an influence on other class teachers' confidence?
Have you had an influence on standards of achievement in art and design?

Advice!

- Maintain a vision.
- Think laterally and work creatively.
- Build positive relationships and empower others.
- Be reflective.
- Be resourceful.
- Be proactive.
- Challenge current practices.
- Be whole school–focused.
- Have a broad local and national perspective.
- Enhance expertise and foster collaborative working.

DEVELOPING A WHOLE SCHOOL POLICY FOR ART AND DESIGN

Art education is an entitlement for every child. In order to provide a broad, balanced and meaningful curriculum for children, it is vital that teachers develop an agreed policy to provide a framework for good practice. Developing a whole school policy for art is a dynamic process that relies on the commitment of the head teacher, the subject leader and the whole staff. Effective policies are developed over a period of time and provide opportunities for evaluation and review. A policy should outline the individual school's approach to teaching and learning in art and provide both a reference point and a set of guidelines to develop sound practice. It should also reflect the school's existing aims and policies on whole school issues such as equal opportunities, planning, differentiation, assessment and reporting.

■ ■ ■ ■ **THE ROLE OF THE ADULT**

Key issues

It is essential that the policy be accessible and supportive. It needs to give clear guidance on agreed principles which reflect the school's individual context. The following areas illustrate the key issues that inform a developing a policy:

1. Rationale
2. Teaching and learning strategies
3. Classroom organisation and management
4. Equal opportunities
5. Planning
6. Assessment and reporting
7. Budget and resources
8. Display and documentation
9. Health and safety
10. Role of the subject leader and staff professional development

Considerations for writing a policy for art

'**Art**' *should be interpreted as* '**art, craft and design**' *throughout.*

Under each of the following headings are the main principles for a school staff to consider when writing a policy for art. There are highlighted questions which subject leaders may wish to use as a basis for whole staff discussion.

1. **Rationale**
   What is the purpose of the policy?
   What is the value of art in the curriculum?
   What are our aims and objectives for teaching art?

The rationale is a statement about the value of art and how it informs children's development. Teachers need to agree on a clear rationale to support learning in and through art. For example:

Learning in and through art is an entitlement to every child. Art should not be a luxury or for the 'chosen few'. Its role is central and its contribution vital. It raises the human condition and enriches personal experience. It gives us a sense of identity, stretches our intellectual and emotional responses and helps us become more flexible and open-minded. Art provides a unique language for expression and communication, helping us to understand the world in which we live and increasing our aesthetic awareness and understanding.

The following points may be used to stimulate discussion:

Art, craft and design are fundamental areas of the curriculum because they

- allow children to explore their experiences of the world, sharpen their perceptions and deepen their intellectual and emotional understanding
- sharpen and focus rational, creative and analytical thought provide a means by which children can communicate their ideas and feelings about their personal, social and cultural worlds

THE ROLE OF THE ADULT

Art, craft and design are essential in a broad and balanced curriculum in

- developing the full variety of human intelligence
- providing a focus for creative thought, aesthetic understanding and action
- the development of a sensitivity to their own and others' responses
- the exploration of ideas, concepts and values
- understanding cultural change and differences
- developing a wide variety of physical and perceptual skills
- developing self-esteem and personal satisfaction

Art, craft and design enables children to

- observe, investigate and interpret personal responses to a variety of experiences and the imagination
- experience the process in which ideas and images are found, refined and developed
- explore the visual and tactile elements of art
- explore, select and control a variety of materials, techniques and processes
- develop an understanding about the work of artists, craftspeople and designers develop a critical vocabulary with which to share their ideas with others about their own work and the work of others

2 Teaching and learning strategies

- *How much time is available for teaching art – per week, per term, per year?*
- *Will art be taught as a discrete area or as part of an integrated curriculum or both?*
- *How are links with other subjects identified?*
- *Will art be taught through group work or whole class activity or both?*

Teachers need to decide how the art curriculum is organised in relation to whole school topic work and how much time is allocated each week to discrete activities in art. There should be a balance between work structured by the teacher and child-initiated work. Emphasis should be placed on first-hand experience, and increasingly children should be encouraged to take responsibility for their own learning. Children should be given the opportunity to work individually, in groups and as a whole class. Clear guidelines may be given about the nature of interaction with children and the appropriate use of language. Specific skills and techniques should be introduced as appropriate.

3 Classroom organisation and management

Which materials will be provided in each class / held centrally?
Is there guidance on the appropriate use of materials?
Will classroom assistants or voluntary helpers be involved in supporting children's learning? If so, in what capacity?
How will information and communication technology (ICT) be used to support work in art?

Decisions need to be made about which materials are provided in each class and which are held as a central resource. Provision needs to be made for activities in

THE ROLE OF THE ADULT

drawing, painting, printmaking, collage, textiles, construction and clay. Children should have access to the appropriate use of information technology to support their work in art. There should be a balance of work in 2D and 3D working on different scales. Teachers may choose to establish a whole school approach to the use and care of materials in order to ensure consistency of practice. It is a statutory requirement that sketchbooks should be introduced at Key Stage 2, but it is a recommendation to establish the use of sketchbooks from Key Stage 1.

4   **Equal opportunities**
    What strategies are used to ensure that all children are supported in developing their understanding of art?
    Is art used as a context to develop awareness of issues relating to gender and cultural diversity?
    Is provision made for children with special educational needs?
    This section should refer to the entitlement of all children to an art curriculum that is rich, varied, challenging and inspiring. Appropriate provision should be made for all children, including children with special educational needs. Art can make a valuable contribution to the education of children with special educational needs: these children derive much benefit from focused experiences in a wide range of materials and processes. Such experiences can raise their self-confidence and enrich their attitudes to themselves and other people. In this way, art has a particular significance for those with special difficulties (physical, sensory, cognitive, emotional and behavioural) as for those with special talents in art. Although work is often differentiated by outcome, individual support and extension activities should recognise differences and inform planning. Emphasis should be placed on valuing children's individual achievements and helping children to experience success. Art offers a unique opportunity for children to explore personal, social and cultural issues in a variety of meaningful contexts.

5   **Planning**
    Is there a common planning format in place for teachers to use?
    What opportunities are there for teachers to share their planning with colleagues?
    How does planning ensure continuity and progression?

    Planning considerations
        children's stages of development / previous experience / intended subsequent experience
        children's interests / home artwork
        cultural environment
        teacher's expertise / confidence
        subject knowledge
        equal opportunities
        time
        resources
        materials
    Questions to consider in planning
        What is the purpose of the activity?
        What ideas / concepts do you want the children to learn?

THE ROLE OF THE ADULT

What experience do they need of materials and processes?
Which skills do they need to develop?
Which elements of the visual language will the children be involved with?
Which artists / craftspeople / designers will they use to inform their work?
What opportunities will they have for evaluation and discussion?

6   **Assessment and reporting (see Chapter 8 for more details on this)**
What are the whole school approaches to assessment?
What strategies can teachers use to make assessments of children's progress in art?
What types of records need to be kept of individual achievements in art?
Is there a whole school portfolio for art?
Do teachers have the opportunity to discuss different levels of achievement with colleagues?
What procedures need to be developed for reporting to parents?
It is vital that the teacher be able to view the whole child in the process of assessment, observing children in different contexts on a continual basis. Assessment is meaningful only if it plays an integral part of the teaching and learning process. Assessment and evaluation are also integral aspects of the art process. Children should be given opportunities for evaluating their own work as well as the work of others. Feedback to children about their own progress in art can inform future planning. Teachers need to develop clear criteria for assessment and decide on strategies for record keeping and reporting. Sketchbooks are a useful source for continual assessment in art; sampling work for portfolios can provide evidence of children's progress.
The teacher's role in assessment involves
   effective planning with clear aims and objectives
   identifying a focus for assessment (e.g., look at how children select and use materials and how they work in a group)
   choosing a small number of children to observe at any one time
   ensuring quality of teacher–child interaction (e.g., making appropriate responses, open-ended questioning, and close observation)
   agreeing on what constitutes 'good' evidence.
Assessment occurs over a period of time, considering a range of work on a continual basis. It relates directly to the ongoing work of the child and can be diagnostic.

7   **Resources and budget**
What resources are available to support units of work?
Is there a balance of first-hand and secondary resources?
Is there a balance of cultural resources?
What opportunities do children have for visits to galleries and museums?
Who is responsible for ordering materials and resources and when?
What funding is available to support staff development?
The range of resources available to teachers for art is variable in quality and cost. Teachers will need to provide a variety of resources to support learning to ensure balance of
   art, craft and design

THE ROLE OF THE ADULT

historical and contemporary
gender
local, national and international

These may be books, postcards, slides, posters, films or artefacts; loans and study collections; visits to galleries and museums; and artists in residence or local groups. In addition to these, each class should have access to a range of natural and made objects (e.g., plants, animals, stones, shells, bark, seed pods, wheels, cogs, kitchen utensils, clothes, musical instruments, toys, containers and textiles). Children need to be encouraged to collect their own resources and have the opportunity to use these in the development of their ideas. It is essential to have an agreed code of practice for the storage and organisation of the resources and how they are made available to individual classes. It is important to ensure that the needs and interests of all children are reflected in the resources shown and used. It is essential to make provision for the purchase of materials and resources in the whole school budget to ensure sufficient access for each class. Issues of funding for staff development need to be taken in the light of the individual school's priorities.

8 **Display**

What are the main principles of display in the school?
Are there guidelines for mounting and presenting work?
Do teachers have responsibility for communal display areas?
How much responsibility are children given for displaying their own work?

Display is always a provocative subject in primary schools! Having a clear policy for display does not need to exclude the teacher's individual personality! It is, however, useful to have a consensus on the functions and principles of display, why it is so important to create a visually stimulating environment for children to learn in and how that is best achieved. Displays of carefully mounted, imaginatively presented work reaffirm its value and make it available to a wider audience. Children's responses should be displayed together with the resource materials and examples of preliminary studies and investigations which support the enquiry. Displays are intended to promote action by posing questions, inviting further investigations and suggesting follow-up activities. Consideration needs to be given to process and product, variety of 2D and 3D, arrangement of work, groupings and focal points, contrasts and similarities, scale, children's work and source material, children's eye level, simple well-written lettering, and children's involvement in mounting and designing a display. Displays of quality help to foster an awareness of, and concern for, the quality of our environment. Children should be encouraged to personalise their surroundings and be helped to develop their own aesthetic judgements.

9 **Health and safety**

Is there a whole school policy on health and safety issues in relation to practical subjects?
Is health and safety awareness part of the children's learning in art?

The health and safety of the children are the responsibility of the class teacher. It is therefore important to ensure that all staff and helpers are confident in the appropriate and correct use of tools. Health and safety issues in art include

THE ROLE OF THE ADULT

correct use of tools (e.g., Stanley knives and glue guns)protecting children's clothing (e.g., from stains)airborne substances (e.g., fixative and clay dust)potential toxic substances in manufactured products (e.g., fungicidal wallpaper paste).

10   **The role of the subject leader**
What are the main responsibilities of the subject leader?
How will the subject leader be supported in their role?
What priorities are in place for staff development?
Are classroom assistants given training to support children in art activities?
What opportunities are there for parent and governor training?

Continual professional development in art is recommended for the subject leader and individual staff. This may include the involvement of parents, governors, classroom assistants and the wider school community.

Aspects of the role of the subject leader are to
- take the lead in policy development and the production of schemes of work designed to ensure progression and continuity in art throughout the school.
- demonstrate good practice in teaching art
- provide guidance to colleagues on developing work
- support colleagues in their development of planning, assessment and reporting procedures
- keep a whole school portfolio of children's work
- delegate responsibility for communal display areas
- monitor progress in art and advise the headteacher on action needed
- coordinate in-service training (InSET) according to staff and individual school needs
- take responsibility for the purchase and organisation of central resources for art
- keep up to date with the developments in art education and disseminate information to colleagues as appropriate.

Procedure for writing a policy

There are many different approaches to writing a school policy for art and the most appropriate will depend on your individual school circumstances. The most successful policies for art are written in collaboration with the whole staff over a period of time and are subject to continual evaluation and review. Ideally, the policy should emerge as part of the whole school development in art. Schools are individual and changing environments that require a commitment to development and progress. However, sometimes policies need to be in place imminently! The following examples show how two schools at different stages of development were able to establish a policy.

Activity: Developing a whole school policy for art and design

Questions for discussion with colleagues

Rationale
What is the purpose of the policy?

What is the value of art in the curriculum?
What are our aims and objectives for teaching art?

Principles of the Teaching and Learning of Art
What are the requirements of the National Curriculum at each Key Stage?
Are sketchbooks in place in both Key Stages?

Strategies for the teaching of art
How much time is available for teaching art – per week, per term, per year?
Will art be taught as a discrete area or as part of topic work or both?
How are links with other subjects identified?
Will art be taught through individual, group work or whole class activity or a combination?

Classroom organisation and management
Which materials will be provided in each class / held centrally?
Is there guidance on the appropriate use of materials?
Will classroom assistants or voluntary helpers be involved in supporting children's learning? If so, in what capacity?
How will information technology be used to support work in art?

Equal opportunities
What strategies are used to ensure that all children are supported in developing their understanding of art?
Is art used as a context to develop awareness of issues relating to gender and cultural diversity?

Special Educational Needs Development
Is provision made for children with special educational needs?

Early years
How is art valued in the early years?
What opportunities are provided across the Foundation stage?

Planning
Is there a common planning format in place for teachers to use?
What opportunities are there for teachers to share their planning with colleagues?
How is planning responsive to children's ideas?

Assessment
What are the whole school approaches to assessment?
What strategies can teachers use to make assessments of children's learning in art?
What types of assessment are made of individual achievements in art?
Are there individual/class/whole school portfolios for art?

Resources
What resources are available for each class?
Is there a balance of art, craft and design from different times and cultures?
What opportunities do children have for visits to galleries and museums?

Documentation and display
What are the main principles of documentation and display in the school?
Are there guidelines for sharing and presenting work?
Do teachers have responsibility for learning walls?
How much responsibility are children given for displaying their own work?

Health and safety
Is there a whole school policy on health and safety issues in relation to practical subjects?
Is health and safety awareness part of the children's learning in art?

Budget

THE ROLE OF THE ADULT

Who is responsible for ordering materials and resources and when?
What funding is available to support staff development?
Continuing professional development and learning (CPDL)
What priorities are in place for staff's CPDL?
Are teaching assistants given training to support children in art activities?
What opportunities are there for parent and governor training?
The role of the subject leader
What are the main responsibilities of the subject leader?
How will the subject leader be supported in their role?
What procedures are in place of reviewing the policy?

EXAMPLES

School A

Developing a policy out of practice

Initial planning
- Discussion between head teacher, subject leader and whole staff
- Art identified in whole school development plan
- Timetable set for InSET day and series of staff meetings
- Curriculum working group established
- Subject leader carries out curriculum and resource audit for art

InSET
- Whole staff InSET day for art
- Discussion about the value of art in the curriculum
- Focus on principles of teaching and learning in art
- Practical workshops looking at different approaches to art
- Overview of National Curriculum requirements

Follow-up
- Each class equipped with a core set of materials and resources
- Curriculum working group identifies and agrees good practice
- Subject leader drafts document for discussion with staff

Staff meetings

Led by the subject leader, the curriculum working group meets to plan a half-termly staff meeting, each focusing on different aspects of teaching and learning in art. Sessions addressed the National Curriculum requirements; using sketchbooks; the visual and tactile elements; using the work of artists, craftspeople and designers; and planning and assessment. Draft a document identifying key issues used as a basis for discussion.

Follow-up
- Each session was subject to review and evaluation by the whole staff.
- Teachers had the opportunity to follow up each session with their own class.
- The curriculum working group meet regularly to review progress.
- Agreed statement of aims and objectives was shared with staff.
- Adjustments were made to the draft policy in the light of practice.

Follow-up by subject leader
- Subject leader writes a draft policy
- Review of existing policies
- Reference made to other whole school policies to ensure consistency
- Draft policy distributed to staff

Implementation
- Staff discuss, evaluate and review policy
- Amendments made
- Discussion about planning and schemes of work
- Agreement to develop units of work in each year group in relation to policy

Follow-up by subject leader
- Adjustments to policy following staff evaluation
- Policy presented to governors for approval
- Collation of plans to formulate schemes of work that show progression and continuity
- Future dates agreed to review policy and schemes of work

School B

Putting a policy into practice

Initial planning
- Discussion between head teacher and subject leader
- Timetable set for three staff meetings
- Subject leader plans a draft framework with appropriate headings
- Review of existing policies
- Key issues identified to be discussed with staff
- Reference made to other whole school policies to ensure consistency
- Draft framework distributed to staff in advance

First staff meeting
- Overview of National Curriculum requirements for art
- Discussion about the value of art in the curriculum
- Agreed statement of aims and objectives
- Discussion about identified key issues

THE ROLE OF THE ADULT

Follow-up by subject leader
- Information collated from staff meeting
- Draft policy developed and presented to staff prior to next meeting

Second staff meeting
- Staff discuss, evaluate and review policy
- Amendments made

Follow-up by subject leader
- Adjustments to policy following staff evaluation
- Policy presented to governors for approval

Third staff meeting
- Discussion about planning and schemes of work
- Agreement to develop units of work in each year group in relation to policy

Follow-up by subject leader
- Collation of plans to formulate schemes of work that show progression and continuity
- Future dates agreed to review policy and schemes of work

Ofsted (Office for Standards in Education, Children's Services and Skills) or School Inspections

Key questions
- What is a school trying to achieve through their arts curriculum? (Intent)
- How is the school's curriculum being delivered? (Implementation)
- What difference is the school's curriculum making? (Impact)

Key judgements
- quality of education
- behaviour and attitudes
- personal development
- leadership and management.

THE ROLE OF THE ADULT

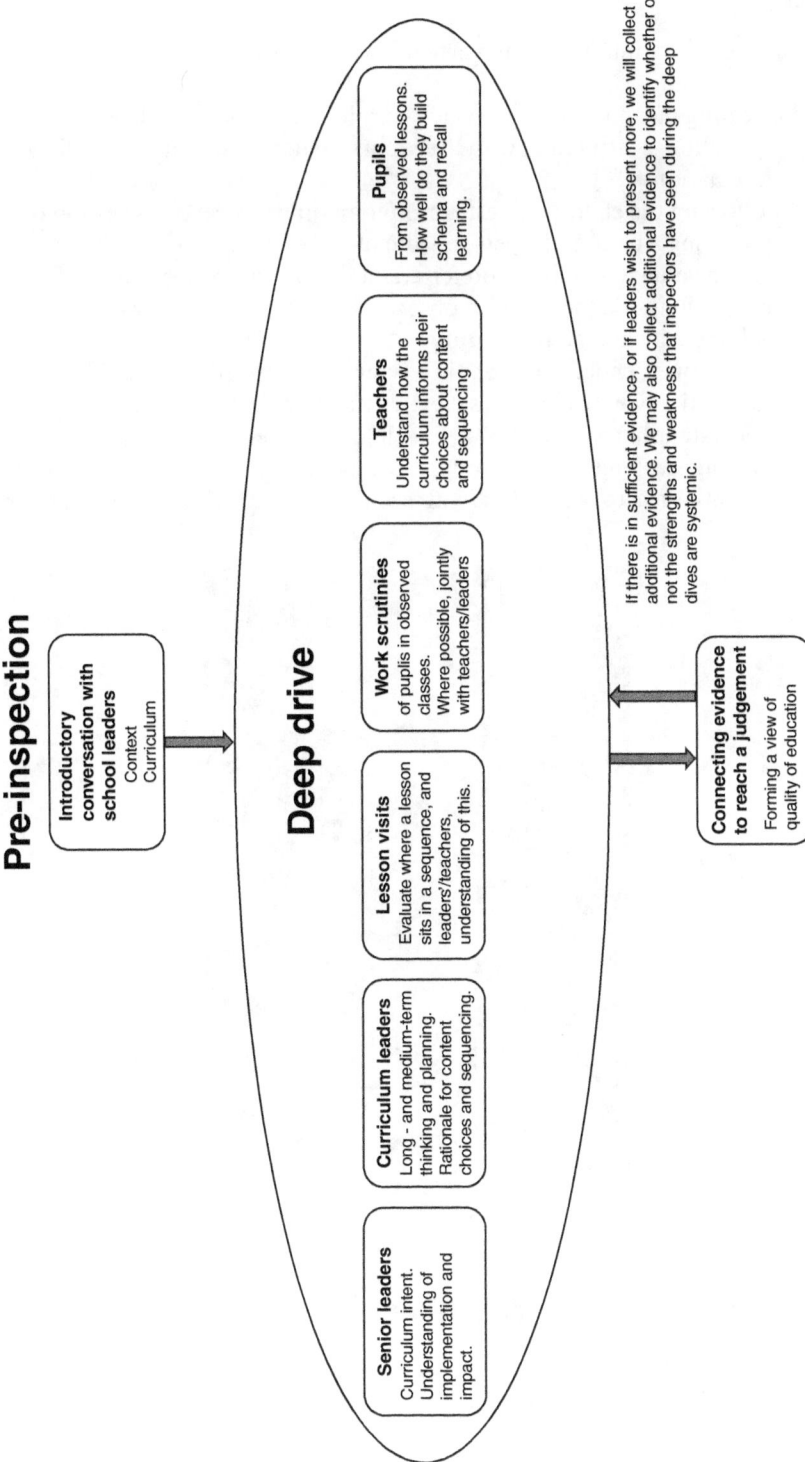

Figure 5.4 Education Inspection Framework 2019

THE ROLE OF THE ADULT

SUMMARY

The role of the adult in teaching art creatively involves

- creating meaningful contexts for learning, inside and outside
- providing a structure with freedom, inviting the child to follow their own fascinations
- following the child's interests or offer an 'up my sleeve' suggestion or both
- providing a choice of open-ended materials
- giving value to children's preferred modes of self-expression
- being alongside the child, to observe and listen, knowing when to step back
- valuing play and active learning
- asking open-ended questions in a genuine conversation about ideas and thoughts
- supporting young children's creativity and critical thinking
- understanding the value of art in children's lives
- making learning visible through documentation
- inviting ways to share work with each other and reflect on the experience

Figure 5.5 Children reflecting together through drawing, Batheaston Primary School

REFERENCES AND FURTHER READING

Edwards, C., Gandini, L., and Forman, G. (1998) *The Hundred Languages of Children: The Reggio Emilia Approach—Advanced Reflections*. Greenwich, CT: Ablex Publishing.

THE ROLE OF THE ADULT

SUGGESTED WEBSITES

https://www.gov.uk/government/publications/national-curriculum-in-england-art-and-design-programmes-of-study
https://www.gov.uk/government/publications/education-inspection-framework
https://www.gov.uk/government/organisations/ofsted
https://www.artscouncil.org.uk/letscreate
https://www.nsead.org/
https://culturallearningalliance.org.uk/
https://www.creativitycultureeducation.org/
https://www.thersa.org/discover/publications-and-articles/reports/arts-cultural-schools
https://64millionartists.com/about/
https://www.bbc.co.uk/arts/sections/get-creative

CHAPTER 6
THE LEARNING ENVIRONMENT FOR ART

A creative environment demonstrates the belief that children have a right to be educated in thoughtfully designed spaces. The experiences of children are enriched if they are provided with rich materials in a studio or 'atelier'. This chapter will show how this can affect an entire school's approach to the construction and expression of thought and learning.

Discussion topics in this chapter will include the following:

- the classroom as studio: the environment as third teacher
- making learning visible
- space, materials and tools
- gallery of learning: displays and documentation as learning resources

In this chapter, we will talk about how to create a stimulating learning environment for primary art education. We will highlight the value offered by a dedicated art room, studio or atelier but also explain how you can make the most of a 'normal' classroom to provide a suitable space for children's art making. The importance of high-quality displays, along with the 'environment as third teacher,' is emphasised. We consider some key materials, tools and techniques and discuss the role of display and documentation.

Providing children with a well-organised and visually exciting environment will help to focus their attention and feed their artistic creativity. It is also important that children have the experience of working alongside artists and using high-quality materials to maximise potential. This chapter will show how the learning environment for art can affect a whole school's approach to art, craft and design.

THE CLASSROOM AS STUDIO: THE ENVIRONMENT AS THIRD TEACHER

The classroom environment can be considered

- a studio where materials are used for various purposes
- a gallery where work is displayed
- a home where the environment is friendly and caring

CHARACTERISTICS OF A CREATIVE LEARNING ENVIRONMENT

Planning opportunities to develop key learning dispositions (e.g., questioning):

Motivation: worthwhile activities, justification, and passion
Inspiration: stimuli, provocations, and rich resources
Collaboration: learning partners, share and build ideas, and open dialogue
Time and space: to play, explore and develop ideas
Autonomy: self-direction, ownership and some choice
Climate: safe, secure to take risks, innovative and risk-laden

Creating a space for exploration and experimentation, as in a creative laboratory or artist's studio, invites children to be curious in their learning through making. Artists' studios are special places and often very personal to the individual artist. A feature of both the 'Being an Artist' workshops and $5 \times 5 \times 5 = creativity$ is the commitment to developing a creative environment as a laboratory for creative participation and critical dialogue between children and adults. The experiences of children are enriched if they are provided with rich materials in a studio or 'atelier'. As in the Reggio Emilia approach, the environment is seen as the 'third educator'. Children can best create meaning and make sense of their world through inhabiting rich environments which support 'complex, varied, sustained, and changing relationships between people, the world of experience, ideas and the many ways of expressing ideas' (Edwards *et al.* 1993).

A creative environment can be designed so that it demonstrates the belief that children deserve to be educated in thoughtfully designed spaces. Gandini *et al.* (2005) explore how the experiences of children interacting with rich materials in the 'atelier' affect an entire school's approach to the construction and expression of thought and learning. An artist's studio space is a good model for this kind of creative 'laboratory' (Bancroft *et al.* 2008: 59). The analysis of space and place in relation to our identities raises questions about who we are and how we become the way we are. In Reggio Emilia, the 'atelierista' has a combined role of artist and teacher, who works closely with children to facilitate and guide their artistic expression and development.

> ... to construct, together with the children, too, an educational learning environment by arranging spaces, furnishings, materials, tools, educational projects, encounters, collaborations, discussions, and exchanges.
> Maria Montessori in Giudici, C. & Rinaldi, C. with Krechevsky, M. (2001)

MAKING LEARNING VISIBLE

Csikszentmihalyi (2002) found that when people find themselves in beautiful settings, they are more likely to find new connections among ideas. It follows that if we provide multi-faceted, multi-layered, visual, tactile, kinaesthetic, emotional spaces, they will be enabling and creative environments for learning. Claxton and Carr (2004) define learning environments as 'prohibiting', 'affording', 'inviting' and 'potentiating'. These

THE LEARNING ENVIRONMENT FOR ART

potentiating environments are those that support and extend learning dispositions – environments where adults and children participate actively, sharing power and responsibility.

The Studio Thinking Framework (Project Zero, see Chapter 3) addresses two aspects of art classrooms: (1) 'studio structures' that art teachers use to organise learning and (2) alongside taught 'studio habits of mind' – dispositions, together with skills and attitudes. The space we provide for children affords the kind of learning that we value – a creative space makes it possible for children to encounter interesting contexts where they can explore diverse ideas and materials to understand 'how children invent autonomous vehicles of expressive freedom, cognitive freedom, symbolic freedom, and paths to communication' (Vecchi 1998).

The atelier serves two functions. First, it provides a place for children to become masters of all kinds of techniques, such as painting, drawing, and working in clay – all the symbolic languages. Second, it assists the adults in understanding processes of how children learn. It helps teachers understand how children invent autonomous vehicles of expressive freedom, cognitive freedom, symbolic freedom, and paths to communication. The atelier has an important, provocative and disturbing effect on old-fashioned teaching ideas ... 'I have discovered how creativity is part of the makeup of every individual, and how the 'reading' of reality is a subjective and cooperative production, and this is a creative act (interview with Vea Vecchi 1998).

The concept of an open, reflective and creative studio environment holds a promise for future communities of creative learning, by enabling children to express their thoughts through a range of creative possibilities while working alongside creative educators and artists in dialogue. This approach has the capacity to feed the creativity of both the children and the adults involved. Many parents and carers may also be artists, and making use of connections within the school community helps to create an inclusive and supportive ethos.

A designated studio space such as Room 13, a learner/artist-led initiative in Caol Primary School in Scotland (and now world-wide), gives learners the opportunity to work alongside artists-in-residence and make art that is engaged with contemporary practices. Children at Caol Primary School may leave lessons to participate in Room 13 activities, provided that they do not fall behind with their other work. Room 13 has taken on a plurality of forms, as other schools have set up their own Room 13s. As one child explains 'What Room 13 does is allow us to take control of our learning' (Danielle Souness, Room 13).

SPACE, MATERIALS AND TOOLS

The learning environment for art should be visually stimulating and inspire children's imaginations. It is possible that a normal classroom can perform some of the functions of an art studio, but this does require careful thinking. Some questions may include the following:

- Are there suitable work/ floor surfaces? A sink?
- Is there good light?

■ ■ ■ ■ **THE LEARNING ENVIRONMENT FOR ART**

■ Can art materials be stored so they are both visible and accessible to children?
■ Is there space to store artwork 'in progress' as it is finished?
■ Is there space for displays, exhibitions?

Activity

Research artists' studios. What would your ideal studio look like? How can you create a stimulating space for art, craft and design in your school?

Suggestions

Take over an empty classroom and transform this into an art studio.
Establish a gallery / exhibition space for your school.
Invite artists to co-design a studio space inside / outside.
Host an exhibition with the local community.
Create a sculpture trail in the school grounds.

Planning spaces, inside and outside, that are flexible and responsive to children's interests and fascinations can capture their imagination and encourage their own lines of enquiry. Carefully chosen resources that reflect children's home culture can provide provocations for problem solving and critical thinking. As adults, we can create opportunities that promote independence, responsibility and autonomy, with meaningful contexts for initiating artwork. By providing a wide range of tools and materials to nurture creativity, we can value children's preferences and entitlement to choose their modes of representation.

■ **Figure 6.1** Window installation, creative space, Batheaston Primary School

THE LEARNING ENVIRONMENT FOR ART

Case study, Batheaston Primary School

The adults followed the children's fascinations and interests to design a creative space for learning. The children used a variety of media and surfaces for making images and creating a new art space. They became very involved in looking through transparent materials and acetate and used them to create a drawing between the inside and outside. Children were enabled to express their thoughts through a range of creative possibilities, working alongside creative educators and artists in dialogue. This environment allowed quieter children to find a voice. Reflection and ongoing analysis will secure children's entitlement to quality experiences and environments.

The 'Being an Artist' workshops afforded opportunities for educators and parents to experience being alongside children in creative enquiries rather than leading or following. Working in the creative space allowed children to explore their imagination, curiosities and fascinations alongside others. Children and families were given many opportunities to be involved in creative activities. In discussion with parents, it was felt that adults' own creativity and the creative dispositions of the adults working alongside the children were important factors in supporting children's creativity.

Figure 6.2 Creativity Fair, Batheaston Primary School

During an annual Creativity Fair, children, parents and grandparents were able to explore a range of materials and processes, working alongside each other to create their own artwork and seeing different ideas emerging from each other's explorations. The Creativity Fairs offered time for families to spend time exploring their creativity together; parents could witness their children's creativity, explore their own creativity, and be alongside their children as partners in exploration and creative expression. The artists lent their skills and dispositions, encouraging the children to use the power of their imaginations and the potential of the materials. Working with different artists in the creative space created opportunities to make visible different forms of expression for thinking and creating. The ongoing documentation not only made the learning visible but also was an invitation to others to explore their own enquiries.

THE LEARNING ENVIRONMENT FOR ART

GALLERY OF LEARNING: DISPLAYS AND DOCUMENTATION AS A LEARNING RESOURCE

What do we mean by documentation?

There is a difference between recording and the process of documentation.
The process of documentation:

- A question guides the observations, often focussed on ways of learning.
- There is collective analysis.
- There are many ways to represent the experience observed.
- Documentation needs to be shared with learners.
- It can inform future plans.

WHO

- Groups of children
- Adults alongside them

WHAT

- Focus on what are they learning and how – both adults and children
- Their engagement, interests and fascinations
- Their interactions and conversations with each other and the adults
- Actions and words
- The context, including any relevant provocations, environment and resources
- The process rather than the product

HOW (the raw material – or documents)

- Sequences of photographs
- Written observations that include description and dialogue BUT not interpretation or assumptions at this stage
- Visual notes (e.g., diagrams, maps, plans and drawings)
- Video or sound recordings

WHY

'By centring our attention on adults' and children's learning, documentation can serve as a valuable teaching, research, and assessment tool.'
(Making Learning Visible, Project Zero, Harvard University)

FOR WHOM

- The children
- The practitioners
- The parents

THE LEARNING ENVIRONMENT FOR ART

- The learning community (of the school, the cluster group, anyone with whom you share the children's learning to inform understanding and practice)

TURNING DOCUMENTS INTO DOCUMENTATION

Documents are transformed into documentation

- When the 'interpretation' of events and learning is included: whereby the learning is 'made visible'.
- Many forms of documentation can be produced from one set of documents, depending on the intended audience.
- Documents do not always turn into documentation – but all source material needs to be kept in a way that it can be sourced when needed.
- Records of reflection sessions and interpretations need to be made at the time of the learning experience or soon after.

Extracts can be taken from the documentation for individual pupil profiles and made into individual learning stories. They can contribute to self-assessment profiles, inform decisions on future staff training needs, and be used in parent information packs. The documentation process is an effective way to share with parents and involve them in their children's learning.

LEARNING WALLS AND DISPLAY

Learning walls of documentation and thoughtful displays of children's work provide an opportunity to share children's creative learning. Displays are resources for learning, not merely decoration. They should be looked at, talked about, used and changed frequently. Displays of carefully mounted and imaginatively presented work reaffirm its value and make it available to a wider audience. Children's responses should be displayed together with the resource materials and examples of preliminary studies and investigations which support the enquiry. Displays are intended to promote action by posing questions, inviting further investigations and suggesting follow-up activities. Displaying children's work has long been recognised as an important part of the role of the teacher and is often seen as recognising children's efforts and achievements. Displays and documentation celebrate teaching and learning and so what is to be displayed, and why, needs careful consideration. Displays can be of 2D or 3D work (or both) and may incorporate audio-visual systems, and the work may be by the children or as a stimulus for learning.

Reference to the school's policy for display, if there is one, will allow any teacher to be confident that their own proposals will fit with the schools' individual ethos and approach. The policy may cover such aspects as the location of displays for certain subject areas and the consequent subject leaders' responsibilities and the types of displays. Reference to the following list of some of the functions of display and the subsequent information and suggestions contained in this section will help you to

■ ■ ■ ■ **THE LEARNING ENVIRONMENT FOR ART**

consider, analyse and evaluate the role of display in relation to your own practice and that of your colleagues.

THE FUNCTIONS OF DISPLAY

There are many ways that displays are used in schools. You may well have come across a wide range of practice already; there are several recent publications which help to contextualise display work as part of a teaching and learning strategy. It's a good idea to photograph your own displays and those of colleagues (with their consent), not only to remember what was achieved in school but also to keep a record of children's work. Photographs are sometimes included formally in schools' assessment, recording and reporting procedures. Recent experiences of teachers during Ofsted (Office for Standards in Education, Children's Services and Skills) inspections indicate that such photographs, properly annotated, are considered invaluable as a record of work and can be used as evidence of children's achievements alongside samples of work.

Displays can
- inform
- consolidate class learning
- enhance children's pride in task outcomes
- excite
- stimulate
- encourage reflection on learning that has taken place
- question and promote discussion
- acknowledge achievement
- identify needs (e.g., be part of the teachers' assessment process)
- reward effort
- invite participation
- link into seasonal activities
- demand engagement
- share and respect children's activities
- assist evaluation
- show internal and external visitors to the class area, including parents, the activities of the class
- foster curiosity about the activities of others
- set quality standards
- relate to any or all areas of the subject curriculum or cross-curricular skills, dimensions and themes
- celebrate religious or other festivals

Displays should
- arouse children's curiosity
- pose questions and stimulate enquiry
- foster participation
- suggest areas for further exploration
- Displays will do this only if they are thoughtfully annotated and interactive.

THE LEARNING ENVIRONMENT FOR ART

DISPLAY INTERPRETATION

Work needs information with it in order for the display to communicate its function effectively. The information which is put up can be very important in helping to communicate the intentions of the display.

Information to be displayed can

- be pre-planned by the teacher with a specific audience in mind
- come about as a result of some interaction between teacher and pupil, essentially reactive and temporary
- be the children's own written communication as they react to stimuli and explain their own collection of work

DISPLAY AND EQUAL OPPORTUNITIES

Experienced teachers often see displaying children's work as part of the strategy for motivating children to learn. Many children's self-esteem and confidence increase when their work is thought of as 'worth putting up' by the teacher, and displaying artwork is no exception. However, when you are thinking about whose work to display, remember that effort is as worthy of reward as ability or competence is.

The type of work to be displayed will need to be sensitively selected to allow the individual child to feel confidence in their own abilities rather than undermined by comparisons with others. Every piece of work which the children produce does not need to be displayed, and you and your colleagues may well have to consider how a rota of displaying work could be made so that all children have something displayed at some time. This is especially important where space for display is restricted. In some schools, English as an additional language will need to be considered for all learning especially written notices and titles so that the approach is genuinely bilingual. The school policy for display can address this and the other issues above.

General guidance for supporting colleagues in successful displays

- Keep it simple.
- Attempt a clean-cut professional look.
- Use neutral and enhancing colours and tones.
- Use appropriate colours which may have relevance to the theme.
- Consider the proportional arrangement of space around the items as well as the items themselves.
- Consider the arrangement of work, groupings and focal points, contrasts and similarities.
- Minimise the use of appropriate adhesives.

THE LEARNING ENVIRONMENT FOR ART

- Avoid overlapping.
- Labels should be clear and consistent and not overlap work with simple well-written lettering.
- Keep borders equal and mounts restrained.
- Avoid cutting around children's images and cutting off corners or mounting work at an angle!
- Find unobtrusive ways of fixing items – try to avoid Sellotape and drawing pins!
- Consider the variety of 2D and 3D.
- Include children's work and source material.
- Consider children's eye level and children's involvement.
- Always be aware of Health and Safety Regulations and fire risk legislation.

If colleagues indicate a need to develop their display skills, you could suggest that they begin by noticing where evidence of display work occurs. For example, there are lots of ideas to be gained from looking at good interesting shop window displays and museum and gallery exhibitions. However, not all ideas which are used in these other settings are appropriate to educational contexts, so you will need to help your colleagues to be selective.

DECIDING ON A FOCUS FOR A DISPLAY

There may be a topic or theme which immediately suggests itself; you may wish to coordinate the display of a range of work in different spaces. Collaboration between colleagues of display work can be extremely rewarding and allows the burden of selection and preparation of work to be shared.

If as the subject leader your post requires you to have an overview of display in your school, it is very important that you and your colleagues undertake the planning, 'thinking through' and visualising of the displays in relation to the teaching and learning objectives and outcomes. Only in this way will the educational nature of the materials and work displayed be able to be maximised.

Consideration should be given to the use of labels and annotations to clearly indicate the content and meaning of the displays, and consider what good practice in display might be. Many teachers have been able to reflect the exploratory and experimental nature of the children's artwork through their annotated displays which have made clear the nature of such work. Thus, the process of working in art is as evident as the product. Colleagues should be encouraged to recognise the importance of high standards of display as part of the overall visual environment in school. This does not necessarily mean always producing complex plans; sometimes quite simple arrangements of objects, artefacts or children's work can 'come alive' and be successfully contextualised through the careful use of captions, labelling and interpretation.

THE LEARNING ENVIRONMENT FOR ART

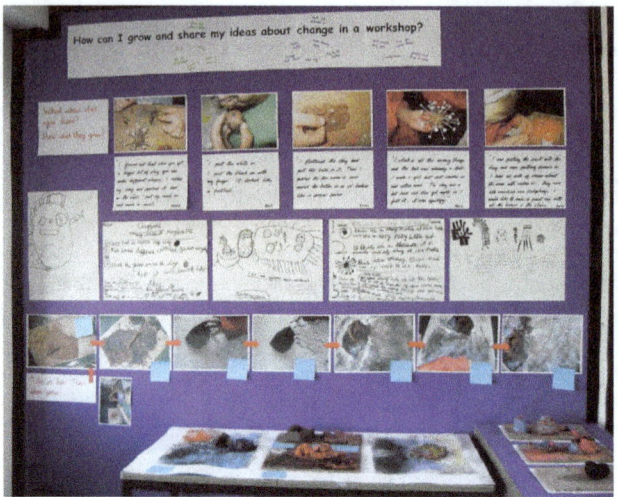

Figure 6.3 Year 2 display at St Vigor and St John Primary School, Chilcompton

Helpful hints

- Look for parallel lines.
- Work with a horizontal or vertical axis.
- Be aware of spaces in between images.
- Plan your display on the floor first.
- Keep lettering at eye height.
- Choose neutral colours for mounting.
- Keep margins to a minimum.

Designing a display

How do you use the space?
How do you lay out the work?
Which colours go well together and enhance the work?
How do you use 3D objects alongside 2D images?
What sort of labelling is appropriate?
Is the display at the children's level?
How do you show the process as well as the outcomes?
Does the display motivate and inspire the children?
Is it interactive? Does it encourage the children to engage with it?
Does it stimulate further questions?
Does it convey information to parents and visitors?

THE LEARNING ENVIRONMENT FOR ART

RESOURCES AND MATERIALS CHECKLIST

Drawing
- Soft pencils 2b/4b/6b
- Coloured pencils
- Charcoal
- Chalk
- Conte crayon
- Biro/felt tips
- Soft pastel
- Oil pastel
- Wax crayon
- Ink
- Selection papers: cartridge/sugar
- Viewfinders
- Putty rubbers
- Pencil sharpeners

Painting
- Ready mixed/powder paint in the double primary system
- Range of brushes/tools
- Range of papers/surfaces
- Water pots
- Sponges
- Flat palettes

Printmaking
- Inking trays
- Inks
- Rollers
- Sponges
- Range of papers
- Found objects
- Pressprint
- Card
- Textured materials
- Brushes
- Mark-making tools
- Scissors/knives
- Cutting mats
- PVA glue
- Glue sticks
- Stencil brushes
- String

Collage
- Scissors/knives
- Cutting mats

THE LEARNING ENVIRONMENT FOR ART

    PVA glue
    Glue sticks
    Range of papers
    Range of fabrics
    Found materials

Textiles
    Fabrics
    Threads
    Yarns
    Ribbons
    Feathers
    Beads
    Found materials
    Needles/pins
    Pipe cleaners
    PVA glue

Construction
    Range of paper/card
    Wood
    Wire
    Pipe cleaners
    PVA glue
    Masking tape
    Scissors/knives
    Cutting mats

Claywork
    Red terracotta clay
    Buff clay
    Grey clay
    Airtight plastic bin
    Modelling boards or cloth
    Modelling tools
    Cutting wire
    Sponges
    If kiln in use:
        Coloured slips
        Transparent glaze
        White opaque glaze

SUMMARY

In this chapter, we have discussed some of the key considerations in providing a creative learning environment for art. We argue that a creative and visually exciting environment is essential to ignite children's artistic motivations.

REFERENCES AND FURTHER READING

Bancroft, S., Fawcett, M., and Hay, P. (2008) *Researching Children Researching the World: 5x5x5=creativity*. Stoke-on-Trent, UK: Trentham Books.

Claxton, G. and Carr, M. (2004) A Framework for Teaching Learning: The Dynamics of Disposition. *Early Years*, 24 (1), 87–97.

Csikszentmihalyi, M. (2002). *Flow*. London: Rider.

Edwards, C., Gandini, L., and Forman, G. (Eds.) (1993) *The Hundred Languages of Children: The Reggio Emilia Approach to Early Years Education*. Norwood, NJ: Ablex Publishing.

Gandini, L., Hill, L., Cadwell, L., and Schwall, C. (Eds.) (2005) *In the Spirit of the Studio: Learning from the Atelier of Reggio Emilia*. New York: Teachers College Press.

Giudici, C. and Rinaldi, C. with Krechevsky, M. (2001) *Making Learning Visible: Children as Individual and Group Learners*. Reggio Emilia RE, Italy: Reggio Children.

Hetland, L., Winner, E., Veenema, S., and Sheridan, K. M. (2007) *Studio Thinking: The Real Benefits of Visual Arts Education*. New York: Teachers College Press.

Vecchi, V. (1998) The Role of the *Atelierista*: An Interview with Leila Gandini. In C. Edwards, L. Gandini, and G. Forman (Eds.), *The Hundred Languages of Children: The Reggio Emilia Approach—Advanced Reflections* (pp. 139–147). Greenwich, CT: Ablex Publishing.

SUGGESTED WEBSITES

https://www.room13scotland.com/room13network.php
https://www.reggiochildren.it/en/

PLANNING ART EXPERIENCES IN THE PRIMARY CURRICULUM

This chapter focuses on inviting children to be part of the planning process for art and design activity. We will discuss different ways that art can be provided for in the curriculum, as both discrete and integrated art experiences. Discrete experiences are valuable in their own right to inform children's learning in and about art and design. Integration provides a way of connecting, deepening and consolidating learning across the curriculum and for maximising available time for art making. We will also look at the notion of responsive planning, building on children's own ideas.

Discussion will include

- responsive planning
- framing learning: integrated and discrete art experiences
- skills development
- connections to wider learning across the curriculum

RESPONSIVE PLANNING: CHILD-INITIATED AND TEACHER-FRAMED ACTIVITIES

> **Activity:** Invite a discussion with your colleagues: 'How can we enable children to initiate and plan their own learning?'

Careful observations of children will provide an insight into their own interests and pre-occupations. It is our role as adults to facilitate and support children's depth of learning. If we respect children and take time to make observations and connections with the children's thinking, we can refine our own efforts in supporting their learning more effectively. Our plans for children's learning can then be responsive to their developing needs and interests.

■ ■ ■ ■ PLANNING ART EXPERIENCES IN THE PRIMARY CURRICULUM

Planning for children's artwork should be responsive and open-ended and needs to be seen in the context of the particular school and class you are working with. They should not be prescriptions or formulae. They should suggest possibilities for ways of working with children with creative provocations and appropriate interventions from adults. Underpinning the approach is the emphasis on children's developing ideas, thoughts and feelings in a supportive environment.

Children will revisit a selection of universal themes through their time in school. These related themes are based on the experience of the human condition: the human form, the environment (natural and built), living things, fantasy and imagination, stories and the abstract.

Once children have been provided with a structure or framework for learning, they can explore the freedom of their own ideas and responses, co-constructing knowledge and testing out hypotheses. Children want to have ownership of the curriculum, working together with teachers as partners in the learning process. As teachers, we need to provide opportunities for exploration, for response and contextualisation of artwork, placing emphasis on confidence building using innovative and imaginative approaches that stimulate the imagination and encourage independent thought.

LEARNING IN, THROUGH AND ABOUT ART

Children learn in, through and about art. Fleming (2012) explains this distinction in connection to the arts more broadly:

> The learning in the arts concept focuses on the **intrinsic** rather than **extrinsic** benefits of engaging in the arts ... At its simplest, learning through, as the preposition suggests, looks beyond the art form itself to **outcomes that are extrinsic,** and often takes places when arts are employed across the curriculum to further learning in other subjects, e.g., the use of visual art to teach reading.
> (Fleming, 2012: 68, emphasis added)

It is useful to discuss the different purposes for learning in art, through art and about art with colleagues, keeping a focus on the value of the activity or experience. Below is a helpful list of some of the benefits and challenges of cross-curricular art learning (NSEAD 2014):

- ■ Literacy, numeracy, information and communication technology (ICT) and Personal Social and Health Education (PHSE) = **integral** to cross-curricular work
- ■ Children can develop a **deeper understanding** of concepts and opportunities for practical application of **skills**

129

PLANNING ART EXPERIENCES IN THE PRIMARY CURRICULUM

- Children are required to develop **research skills**
- Teacher becomes a **learning partner**
- Children's questions, ideas and outcomes are valued to enable **personalised learning**

> **Questions for consideration**
>
> 1 How will we decide on a theme together?
> 2 How can we involve the children's decisions?
> 3 Will the children work individually or collaboratively or both?
> 4 What shared experiences can we plan together?
> 5 What skills, knowledge and understanding do we want to explore?
> 6 What experts from the community (e.g., artists) can we invite to the school?
> 7 How can we make the project personally meaningful? To each child? To the teachers?
> 8 How can the children share their learning?

STARTING POINTS FOR PLANNING

Here are some starting points that might help you decide what you and the children will focus on:

- responding to the **children's interests** (e.g., nature and superheroes)
- exploring a type of **media** (e.g., paint and charcoal)
- looking at an **artist's work** (e.g., your favourite artist's work)
- focusing on a **theme** (e.g., people and fantasy)
- focusing on a **cross-curricular theme** (e.g., environment and stories)
- developing a **skill or technique** (e.g., drawing and printmaking)
- responding to a planned **trip/experience** (e.g., the local park and forest)
- exploring something **incidental** (e.g., the weather and the news)

PLANNING

The main characteristics of planning which have a positive effect on children and their achievement are where

1 planning is responsive to children's interests
2 planning reflects the aims, principles and ethos of the school
3 planning that has a strong sense of involvement and shared ownership by teachers
4 planning shows the complexity and continuous nature of the creative process
5 planning feeds into ongoing assessment and evaluation, alongside children.

■ ■ ■ ■ PLANNING ART EXPERIENCES IN THE PRIMARY CURRICULUM

■ **Figure 7.1** Children exploring Edwina Bridgeman's exhibition, Victoria Art Gallery, Bath

---

Planning art and design activities: Questions to consider

Project/Theme
What range of starting points is relevant to the children's experience?

Aims and Objectives
What skills, knowledge ideas or concepts do you want the children to learn? In the long term? In the short term?

Possible Art Activities
What possible art activities can you develop through this theme? What is the purpose of these activities? To observe, remember or imagine; to tell a story; to illustrate and communicate ideas; to express feelings; to explore materials and the visual language; or to explore and develop ideas?
Are these activities appropriate to the age and experience of the children?
How do they build on the children's previous experience?
How will you structure the activities to ensure a meaningful sequence of work?

Resources
What visual resources do you need to collect?
What opportunities will you give to the children to gather their own resources?
Which artists, craftspeople or designers will you use to inform the children's work? Have you considered the balance of work from different times, cultures and contexts?

Materials
Which materials will you provide?
What skills and techniques will the children need to facilitate this experience?
What skills and techniques will the children learn through engaging in this experience?

PLANNING ART EXPERIENCES IN THE PRIMARY CURRICULUM

Organisation
How will you organise the activities in the classroom?
How will the children be organised – individually, in groups, as a class?
Who else will be facilitating this experience – parent helpers, classroom assistants? What responsibility will you give to the children for organising their own working space, materials and resources?
How will you introduce the activity?
What use of language will you use to support and extend the children's learning?
How will you plan for differentiation?

Development
What possibilities are there for developing further learning in art and design?
What possibilities are there for developing further learning across the curriculum?

Review, Assessment and Recording
What opportunities will there be to review the children's achievements? How will you display and present the children's work to record process as well as product?

The most important aspect of planning is to consider the habits of mind and creative processes that children will be engaged in:

Art

create

see explore think

experiment investigate

imagine make question feel

respond look collaborate design

enquire record construct connect

play observe identify view

discover

critique understand review

evaluate

■ ■ ■ ■ PLANNING ART EXPERIENCES IN THE PRIMARY CURRICULUM

■ **Figure 7.2** Children exploring paint and mixed media on canvas

Key skills	Art Form	Criteria	Media	Universal theme	Processes	Elements
Enquiry Curiosity Questioning Listening	Art, craft and design	Personal experience and personal response	Drawing	Fantasy	Exploration	Line
Problem Solving Reasoning Making Connections Lateral Thinking	Dance	Ideas and meanings	Painting	Abstract/ Formal	Observation	Tone
Social Skills Managing Feelings Empathy Collaboration	Music	Media and process	Printing	Human Form	Expression	Pattern
Evaluation Reflection Review Communication	Drama	Context / Genre	3D / Sculpture	Natural / Urban Environment	Design	Shape
Motivation Perseverence Self Awareness Resilience	Story	Historical, Cultural Contemporary links	Collage	Story / Narrative	Narrative	Colour
Apply Knowledge Undestanding Being Different Sharing Ideas	Poetry	Approaches and ways of working	Textiles	Festivals and Celebrations	Illustration	Form
Creativity Imagination Value And Purpose Independence	Architecture	Universal theme	Digital media	Flora and Fauna	Critical study	Texture

Dr Penny Hay 2020

■ **Figure 7.3** A Planning Matrix to adapt for your school

PLANNING ART EXPERIENCES IN THE PRIMARY CURRICULUM

AN OPEN FRAMEWORK FOR PLANNING

In the early years, the 'Expressive Arts' involves enabling children to explore and play with a wide range of media and materials as well as providing opportunities and encouragement for sharing their thoughts, ideas and feelings through a variety of activities in art, music, movement, dance, role-play, and design and technology. The key characteristics for learning in the early years – active learning; creating and thinking critically; playing and exploring – are central to good practice in learning in and through art, craft and design.

The art, craft and design curriculum for Key Stage 1 and Key Stage 2 introduces children to a broad range of knowledge, understanding and skills. The National Curriculum specifies three areas of making that pupils should be taught at Key Stage 1 and Key Stage 2 as a basic entitlement – drawing, painting and sculpture – to be complemented by other techniques. Children are invited to engage in drawing, painting, sculpture, printmaking, craft, collage, textiles, photography, film and digital media as well as mixed media and installation art. Learning in, through and about art, craft and design places emphasis on creative skills underpinned by a knowledge-rich curriculum. It is important to stress that progression in art, craft and design is not linear but more like a spiral, where children are gaining an increasing repertoire of concepts and skills. Children's knowledge, understanding and skills are developed through their experience of making and talking about art, craft and design, encompassing the following processes:

- **Knowledge and understanding** – responding to a wide range of artists, designers, craftspeople and architects from different times, cultures and contexts
- **Generating ideas** – exploring possibilities and expressing ideas, thoughts and feelings and using a sketchbook to research and record ideas
- **Making** – exploring qualities of different media and processes and transforming materials to construct meaning
- **Evaluating** and reflecting on the learning process and using the language and vocabulary of art, craft and design

---

National Curriculum in Art and Design: Aims

The National Curriculum for art and design aims to ensure that all pupils

- produce creative work, exploring their ideas and recording their experiences
- become proficient in drawing, painting, sculpture and other art, craft and design techniques
- evaluate and analyse creative works using the language of art, craft and design
- know about great artists, craft makers and designers and understand the historical and cultural development of their art forms

National Curriculum in Art and Design: Purpose of study

Art, craft and design embody some of the highest forms of human creativity. A high-quality art and design education should engage, inspire and challenge pupils, equipping

PLANNING ART EXPERIENCES IN THE PRIMARY CURRICULUM

them with the knowledge and skills to experiment, invent and create their own works of art, craft and design.

As pupils progress, they should be able to think critically and develop a more rigorous understanding of art and design. They should also know how art and design both reflect and shape our history and contribute to the culture, creativity and wealth of our nation.

National Curriculum in Art and Design: Breadth of Study

- exploring a range of starting points
- working individually and collaboratively
- using a range of materials and processes in 2D and 3D on different scales, including ICT
- investigating art, craft and design in the community and from different times and cultures

Subject content

Key Stage 1

Pupils should be taught
- to use a range of materials creatively to design and make products
- to use drawing, painting and sculpture to develop and share their ideas, experiences and imagination
- to develop a wide range of art and design techniques in using colour, pattern, texture, line, shape, form and space
- about the work of a range of artists, craft makers and designers, describing the differences and similarities between different practices and disciplines and making links to their own work

Key Stage 2

Pupils should be taught to develop their techniques, including their control and use of materials, with creativity, experimentation and an increasing awareness of different kinds of art, craft and design.

Pupils should be taught

- to create sketchbooks to record their observations and use them to review and revisit ideas
- to improve their mastery of art and design techniques, including drawing, painting and sculpture with a range of materials (e.g., pencil, charcoal, paint and clay)
- about great artists, architects and designers in history

SUMMARY

This chapter has emphasised the importance of inviting children to be part of the planning process for art and design activities and planning in response to the children's own ideas. Art can be provided for in the curriculum, as both discrete and integrated art experiences. Skills development in each aspect of art, craft and design is key to developing children's confidence as artists and makers. Art invites connections to wider learning across the curriculum, learning in, through and about art, craft and design.

REFERENCES AND FURTHER READING

Fleming, M. (2012) *The Arts in Education: An Introduction to Aesthetics, Theory and Pedagogy*. London: Routledge.

Laevers, F. (2015) *Making Care and Education More Effective Through Wellbeing and Involvement: An Introduction to Experiential Education*. Research Centre for Experiential Education, University of Leuven Belgium.

NSEAD (2014). https://www.nsead.org/

CHAPTER 8
EVALUATION AND ASSESSMENT IN PRIMARY ART

This chapter will offer creative and formative approaches to assessment where children are given responsibility for their own evaluation. Discussion will include

- why and how you can assess art
- the relationship between planning and assessment
- review and evaluation processes
- formative assessment
- sketchbooks and portfolios
- focus areas for assessment
- reporting to parents and carers

WHY AND HOW CAN YOU ASSESS ART?

Assessment is a holistic practice and happens through conversation. The role of the teacher is to introduce key skills and materials to children, elicit their ideas and engage children in open-ended possibilities with no prescriptive outcomes in a positive and nurturing environment. Assessment can be integrated into the teaching and learning process to value the children's achievements rather than attainment. There is a need for 'subtle and skilled use of assessment' on the part of the teacher (Ofsted 2012, p. 3). The role of the teacher is in dialogue, alongside the child's learning in art, craft and design, giving constructive and positive feedback rather than purely assessing the outcome, which can be subjective. The most important aspect of assessment is the child's own reflection on their learning and what they might do next or do differently.

The learner's ability to take control over their own learning processes (metacognition) allows children to

- integrate prior and new knowledge
- acquire and use a range of learning skills

DOI:10.4324/9781315691114-8

EVALUATION AND ASSESSMENT IN PRIMARY ART

- solve problems individually and in groups
- think carefully about their successes and failures
- accept that learning involves uncertainty and difficulty.

This diagram sets out the relationship between assessment in art and the whole curriculum.

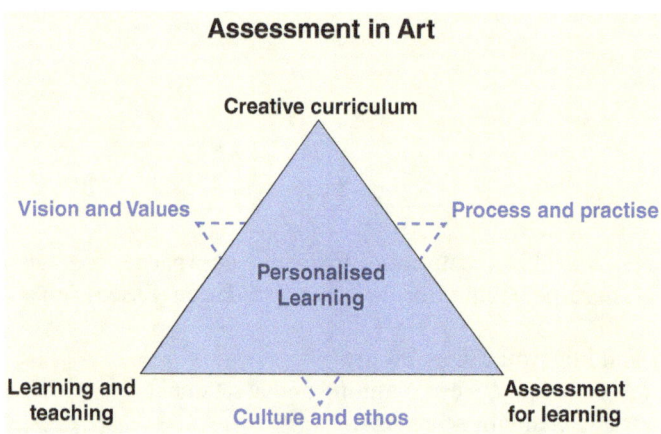

Figure 8.1 Sketchbooks, Year 2

■ ■ ■ ■ **EVALUATION AND ASSESSMENT IN PRIMARY ART**

The relationship between planning and assessment in art and design

Guidance for teachers:

Planning considerations

- children's stages of development / previous experience / intended subsequent experience
- children's interests / 'non-school' artwork
- cultural environment
- teacher's expertise / confidence
- National Curriculum requirements
- equal opportunities
- time
- resources

There is a need for a balance between work that is

- teacher structure / child-initiated
- discrete / topic-based
- individual / group / class
- 2D / 3D / small-scale / large-scale
- art / craft / design
- observational / expressive / narrative / illustrative
- evaluating their own / others' work
- using contemporary / historical sources
- cross-cultural

REVIEW AND EVALUATION PROCESSES

Review and evaluation processes relate directly to the teachers' assessment of their own practice. It involves a review of the learning that has taken place in relation the activity. For the child, assessment occurs over a period of time alongside the teacher, considering a range of work on a continual basis. It relates directly to the previous work of the child and can be diagnostic.

Activity

Questions for colleagues
What assessment procedures are in place for art and design?
Do assessments inform future teaching?
Is assessment used to monitor achievements and progress?
How are children involved in self-assessment tasks?
What evidence is collected to support teachers' assessments?
How are the outcomes of assessment reported to parents?

EVALUATION AND ASSESSMENT IN PRIMARY ART

FORMATIVE ASSESSMENT

Teachers can make informed judgements about the progress children have made in learning **skills and techniques**, in developing **attitudes and concepts** and acquiring new **knowledge and understanding**.

Marking or grading children's art has no place in the primary school. Assessment criteria can relate directly to the teacher's own planning in relation to the National Curriculum. It is good practice to share these criteria with children and to engage them in the process of reflection and evaluation of their own learning and each other's work, creating a positive ethos to share ideas and artwork.

Ongoing formative teacher assessment happens during art sessions, with the children engaged in the process, and is integral to the art making. At the heart of assessment is critical discourse – children and their teachers in dialogue about making art, each responding positively and sensitively in a way that develops the children's thinking. Formative assessment can be used to guide the progress of individual children and may include the following:

- individual discussions with children evaluating their own work alongside the teacher
- focus group discussions in the context of a practical task
- peer-to-peer discussions
- whole class discussions reviewing and evaluating work
- discussions with other teachers to share learning
- process and preparatory work
- class displays of outcomes, images and artefacts
- written evidence and children's own views
- sketchbooks and portfolios
- whole school portfolios

SKETCHBOOKS AND PORTFOLIOS AS DIAGNOSTIC TOOLS

An example of using sketchbooks

Art has traditionally has been measured by a sense of progression from less sophisticated to more skilful art production. However, art education in a contemporary context is centred upon creative and critical thinking, reflection and the transformative power of art. Mere lists of visual elements, media or domains are insufficient to reflect the complexity of learning in art and design. The notion of linear progression is misleading, especially in relation to art making, as the creative process itself highlights the value of exploration and unexpected outcomes. Giving children the time and freedom to explore ideas without judgement of failure can open up spaces of possibility for them that otherwise would have been closed down by outcome-led approaches to teaching and learning. Self-expression and creativity can be finely balanced with an unfolding repertoire of skills, concepts and knowledge in relation to art and design as a discipline.

■ ■ ■ ■ EVALUATION AND ASSESSMENT IN PRIMARY ART

Sketchbooks are important for children to develop and record ideas, review and reflect on their work, and maintain a dialogue about their ongoing themes and fascinations. Giving the children the opportunity to annotate their work is an important aspect of developing an ongoing dialogue with them and gives the teacher insight into their ideas. Sketchbooks can create a shared point for conversation about the children's art making and offer a diagnostic tool for the teacher to support the child's individual learning pathway. They help to make the learning visible and act as an integral tool for both the expression of ideas and meaning-making. Using sketchbooks opens up a dialogue about children's future explorations and artwork and provides a point of reference to share ideas. Children take great pride in keeping their sketchbooks and will share these with peers, teachers, parents and carers. Sketchbooks and ongoing artwork can be displayed as documentation of processes rather than solely as the end products.

> Through observing children engaged in processes of making art, I have seen the children in a different light, I have noticed their own interests and self-chosen themes, and how they have used their imagination to explore ideas.
> – Year 4 teacher, St Andrew's Primary School, Bath

Given time to develop their thoughts and ideas through using their sketchbooks to reflect on and process their experiences, children are encouraged to express their thoughts and feelings. Giving children the freedom to follow their own lines of enquiry, supported and scaffolded appropriately, increases motivation, engagement and personal achievement.

> It's good because you can look back and see what you've done. It's also nice to see other people's ideas, it made me think about different kinds of art too.
> – Year 5 child, Batheaston Primary School

■ **Figure 8.2** 'Being an Artist' workshops, discussion on using sketchbooks, Reception to Year 6

EVALUATION AND ASSESSMENT IN PRIMARY ART

CHILDREN REVIEWING THEIR WORK TOGETHER

Ideally, assessments are made by, with and alongside the child. Focus can be given to individual and collaborative work in a range of media and how children use their books to review ideas, making connections with the work of other artists. Assessment can be purposeful if it draws on the observation of children initiating their own learning with adults supporting the child in developing their artwork with sustained interest and enquiry. Subtle and strategic use of assessment, focused on individual children's developing confidence and competence in art and design, is vital.

Focus areas for assessment

Creative knowledge and understanding, including children's ideas about art, artists, designers and makers
Creative analysis, including critical skills, decision making, evaluating and reflecting
Creative development, skills, techniques and making
Creative use of media, including different materials and processes
Creative inspiration, observation, imagination and generating ideas
Creative process of working, including using a sketchbook

Establishing criteria

It is important to establish clear objectives for the children's learning in order to identify assessment opportunities within any activity.
   What do we want the children to learn?

- to make personal responses to ideas and themes using observation, memory and imagination
- to gather and use resources and to collect visual information
- to research and develop ideas
- to use appropriate media and processes
- to develop a 'visual language'
- to review and modify their work
- to develop an awareness and understanding about the different kinds of art, craft and design
- to apply their knowledge and understanding of other artists, craftspeople and designers to inform their own work.

Questions to consider

- What is the purpose of the activity?
- What ideas / concepts do you want the children to learn?
- What experience do they need of materials and processes?
- Which skills do they need to develop?
- Which elements of the visual language will the children be involved with?
- Which artists / craftspeople / designers will they use to inform their work?
- What opportunities will they have for evaluation and discussion?

EVALUATION AND ASSESSMENT IN PRIMARY ART

What counts as evidence?

Assessment based on judgement arrived at through accumulative evidence

- teacher observation and notes
- child / teacher discussion (individual / group)
- child / child discussion (individual / group)
- teacher / teacher discussion
- process work / preparatory work
- outcomes / images / artefacts
- written evidence / child's own view
- sketchbooks / portfolios

The teacher's role in assessment

- effective planning with clear aims and objectives
- identifying a focus for assessment (e.g., look at how children select and use materials and how they work in a group)
- choosing a small number of children to observe at any one time
- ensuring quality of teacher–child interaction (e.g., making appropriate responses, open-ended questioning and close observation)
- agreeing on what constitutes 'good' evidence

Questioning

The role of questioning is central in eliciting an insightful response for a child, and open-ended questions especially open up meaningful conversations about learning. It's also important that children be allowed to ask their own questions.

QUESTIONS AND STATEMENTS TO FOCUS THE ASSESSMENT PROCESS

- Tell me about that you are making and what inspired you.
- What have you discovered about the materials and techniques you are using?
- Tell me about what you really enjoyed or found challenging.
- What would you like to explore more of? What might you do next?
- What did you learn? (About the subject, the medium, the process, technique, yourself, other artists?)

Activity: Watch the video 'Austin's Butterfly' (see https://www.youtube.com/watch?v=hqh1MRWZjms) and consider the following question: How did the teacher facilitate peer assessment? What might you do differently?

EVALUATION AND ASSESSMENT IN PRIMARY ART

Exemplar Assessment Sheet Art Curriculum	Creative process
Each child should be supported to	Each child should be given the opportunity to
■ know about different materials, tools, techniques and formal elements ■ describe, interpret and explain the work, ideas and working practices of artists, craftspeople, architects and designers from different cultures, times and contexts, including contemporary artists ■ talk about the materials, techniques and processes they have used, using an appropriate vocabulary. ■ demonstrate how to safely use some of the tools and techniques they work with	■ engage in the creative process, following their fascinations ■ understand how ideas are generated and developed through the art-making process ■ develop their experience and knowledge of different materials, processes and techniques ■ work at different scales, individually and collaboratively ■ discuss and evaluate their own work ■ share their journey and outcomes with others

REPORTING TO PARENTS AND CARERS

Art subject leaders may encourage the whole class and whole school portfolios to include a range of work from children. This can act as a reference to teachers in planning and recording the breadth and balance of the art curriculum. There is a statutory requirement that teachers make an annual statement about each child's progress. The National Curriculum has end-of-key-stage descriptions that can be adapted to your setting:

- skills and use of media
- conceptual development
- attitudes
- knowledge and understanding
- critical skills

Some suggested statements for reporting

- Child X independently develops a range of ideas which show curiosity, imagination and originality.
- Child X investigates, researches and test ideas and plans using sketchbooks and a variety of media.
- Child X analyses, evaluates and reflects on the creative process.
- Child X shows how this is informed by understanding art, craft and design in different contexts.

HOW CAN YOU ASSESS CREATIVITY IN ART?

Drawing on Desailly's (2012) 'Key Elements of Creativity,' these help to focus the evaluation and assessment of creativity in art:

EVALUATION AND ASSESSMENT IN PRIMARY ART

1. generating new ideas
2. applying known skills and ideas in different contexts
3. taking other people's ideas or starting points and moving them on or personalising them
4. communicating ideas in interesting or varied ways
5. putting different or disparate ideas together to make something new
6. working towards a goal or set of goals
7. evaluating their own or others' work
8. adapting and improving on their work in the light of their own or others' evaluations

St Vigor and St John School, Chilcompton have been working on 'Learning Habits' from Reception to Year 6. These inform the whole curriculum but are exemplified in art:

Learning Habits

I can be curious	**I can make links**	**I can communicate**
playing	comparing	effectively and efficiently telling
noticing	pattern seeking	articulating in specific &
observing	seeing relationships	approriate forms
questioning	identifying similarities & differences	celebrating
investigating	making connections	defining
wondering	applying & using learning	translating
possibility thinking - 'what if...?'	using K & u in new contexts	using methods with fluency
		'100 languages'

I can analyse	**I can grow ideas**	**I can evaluate**
reasoning	forming new ideas	reviewing
inferring	making meaning	assessing
deducing	synthesising	judging
justifying	formulating	reflecting
interpreting	hypothesising	giving an opinion
distilling		justifying
		making conclusions

Figure 8.3 Learning Habits, St Vigor and St John School, Chilcompton

Similarly, Twerton Infant School worked together as a staff to identify the key habits of mind of learners.

'Twerton Infant School have been members of the 5 × 5 × 5/House of Imagination project – creativity in the Early Years for many years. During this project, we have researched ways to encourage positive learning attitudes and develop skills of research, investigation and problem solving in young children. The positive gains we have seen in children's attainment have encouraged us to utilise our research to invigorate our teaching and learning practice throughout the Foundation Stage (and into Key Stage 1). We are developing and testing this philosophy by reassessing the content and delivery of the whole curriculum. The main features of this strategy are the following:

- children having an active part in initiating and planning their own learning with teachers collaborating as partners
- enabling children to review their learning and participate in planning the next steps
- making key skills, such as collaboration and problem solving, central to our teaching and learning
- making the existing learning environment much more flexible and exploring different working areas both inside and out
- being proud of where we live and using the local areas as starting points for projects
- making the structure of the day less constricting to allow for longer periods of concentrated involvement
- creating a learning community involving parents and the wider community and celebrating this learning through photographic displays of learning in action

We can now see evidence of

- children developing powerful skills in questioning, problem solving and investigating. They tell us what they want to learn!
- children in control and excited by their learning
- collaboration with both children and adults – working together to solve problems, share resources and ask each other's opinion and advice
- children believing in creative possibilities – an 'anything is possible' culture
- parental support understanding and interest in what children are doing
- children's concentration and interest increased
- children's improved behaviour and increased self-esteem
- children's improved attainment now measurable in Foundation Stage Profile (and Key Stage 1 Standard Assessment Tasks results which are now above the national average)

We understand that our children need to be actively involved in their learning, both emotionally and physically. We aim to instil the positive attitudes and skills to empower our children to become life-long learners. We believe our developing practice enhances our school's promise to children and parents.

The Foundation Stage Curriculum offers the opportunity to build a child's creative choices into a developmental learning journey. Watching and documenting how children respond to certain stimuli allows the educators to personalise the learning for the child. It is the educator's job to ask the right questions of the child and provide further learning stimuli based on their answers. Young children should be encouraged to develop a portfolio of their own creative work, which can be shared with peers and parents and travel with them as they move to primary school.'

– *Jayne Rochford Smith, Reception teacher*

EVALUATION AND ASSESSMENT IN PRIMARY ART

Here is the overview of their learning habits of mind that also inform the whole school curriculum:

YEAR R		KEY SKILL	'I' STATEMENT
Independent enquirers	Enquire	Be curious	I am curious about new things.
		Question	I ask questions using what, when, where.
	Problem-solve	Plan	I can plan where I will work and what I will do.
		Make choices	I can make a choice from a limited selection of resources.
		Reason	I can give a simple reason for an action.
	Apply knowledge	Form opinions	I can give a simple opinion of my own.
		Apply knowledge	I can make links to find simple relationships between objects.
Reflective learners	Evaluation	Reflect	I can tell someone what I've been doing.
		Revise	I can tell someone what I would do differently next time.
Creative thinkers	Creativity	Use imagination	I can use my imagination in role-play.
		Lateral thinking	I can suggest a way to solve a problem.
		Meta-learning	I can tell someone what I'm doing.
Self-managers	Motivation	Persevere	I stick at a short task until I have finished it.
		Manage distractions	I can stay on task when working in a group with an adult.
		Set goals	I can work with an adult to set myself a small challenge.
	Emotional skills	Be self-aware	I can tell others what I enjoy.
		Manage my feelings	I know what to do if I feel upset.
		Understand others' feelings	I can recognise some simple emotions in other people.
Team workers	Social skills	Be independent	I can tidy up at the end of an activity.
		Collaborate, value & support others	I can take turns in an activity.
		Communicate	I talk to others.
YEAR 1		KEY SKILL	'I' STATEMENT
Independent enquirers	Enquire	Be curious	I am curious about new things and share this with someone else.
		Question	I ask questions using how & why.
	Problem-solve	Plan	I can plan a simple sequence of instructions.
		Make choices	I can make a choice from a selection of resources.
		Reason	I can give a reason for an event or action.
	Apply knowledge	Form opinions	I can give a simple opinion of my own and explain why.
		Apply knowledge	I can sort objects into a variety of groups and give reasons.

EVALUATION AND ASSESSMENT IN PRIMARY ART

Reflective learners	Evaluation	Reflect	I can tell someone what I have learnt.
		Revise	I can try a different approach if something doesn't work.
Creative thinkers	Creativity	Use imagination	I can use my imagination to make things.
		Lateral thinking	I can suggest a variety of ways to solve a problem.
		Meta-learning	I can tell someone why I'm doing something.
Self-managers	Motivation	Persevere	I keep trying when an adult encourages me.
		Manage distractions	I can listen, learn and think at carpet time.
		Set goals	I can set myself a target.
	Emotional skills	Be self-aware	I can tell someone how I am feeling.
		Manage my feelings	I stop and think before acting.
		Understand others' feelings	I can recognise a range of emotions in other people.
Team workers	Social skills	Be independent	I can choose resources from a selection provided.
		Collaborate, value & support others	I can share ideas and listen to a partner.
		Communicate	I can add detail to interest my listener.
		Listen	I listen carefully to instructions and follow them.

YEAR 2		KEY SKILL	'I' STATEMENT
Independent enquirers	Enquire	Be curious	I am curious about new things and ask questions to find out more.
		Question	I can suggest the question when given an answer.
	Problem-solve	Plan	I can write simple instructions for someone else to follow.
		Make choices	I can make a choice from a limited selection of methods.
		Reason	I can explain a simple word problem showing my thinking.
	Apply knowledge	Form opinions	I can give two different opinions and say which one I agree with.
		Apply knowledge	I can make links to give a simple description of similarities & differences.
Reflective learners	Evaluation	Reflect	I can share my learning with the class.
		Revise	I can make changes to my work and explain my reasoning.
Creative thinkers	Creativity	Use imagination	I can use my imagination to generate lots of ideas.
		Lateral thinking	I can suggest ways to solve a range of problems.
		Meta-learning	I can tell someone what I am learning.

EVALUATION AND ASSESSMENT IN PRIMARY ART

Self-managers	Motivation	Persevere	I keep going when things are hard.
		Manage distractions	I don't let others distract me when I am working independently.
		Set goals	I can review my achievements against success criteria.
	Emotional skills	Be self-aware	I understand my actions can affect other people.
		Manage my feelings	I will try new things with support even when I feel apprehensive.
		Understand others' feelings	I can describe someone else's feelings.
Team workers	Social skills	Be independent	I can collect all the resources I need from around the classroom.
		Collaborate, value & support others	I can work with people chosen by my teacher.
		Communicate	I can give an opinion.
		Listen	I know how to actively listen, think and share ideas.

YEAR 3		KEY SKILL	'I' STATEMENT
Independent enquirers	Enquire	Be curious	I am curious about new things and ask questions at home to find out more.
		Question	I can suggest a question which can be investigated.
	Problem-solve	Plan	I can plan and finish a simple task within a set time.
		Make choices	I can make a choice from a range of methods.
		Reason	I can solve two step word problems showing my thinking.
	Apply knowledge	Form opinions	I can give two different opinions and say which one I agree with and why.
		Apply knowledge	I can see relationships between things and explain my ideas in a group.
Reflective learners	Evaluation	Reflect	I can take time to consider my experience and what I need to do next.
		Revise	I can make check and edit my work.
Creative thinkers	Creativity	Use imagination	I can use my imagination to improvise.
		Lateral thinking	I can think of different ideas and possibilities when solving problems.
		Meta-learning	I can improve my learning by imitating others.
Self-managers	Motivation	Persevere	I keep going and look for new ways to solve problems.
		Manage distractions	I complete my work in the time allowed.
		Set goals	I can set and review targets for my learning.
	Emotional skills	Be self-aware	I can talk about my attitudes to learning.
		Manage my feelings	I will try new things even when I feel apprehensive.
		Understand others' feelings	I can appreciate a range of feelings, emotions and viewpoints.

EVALUATION AND ASSESSMENT IN PRIMARY ART

Team workers	Social skills	Be independent	I listen and follow instructions independently.
		Collaborate, value & support others	I can work in a team making sure everyone has a turn at speaking.
		Communicate	I can give an opinion and explain it.
		Listen	I listen, then comment on what I have heard, asking relevant questions.
YEAR 4		KEY SKILL	'I' STATEMENT
Independent enquirers	Enquire	Be curious	I can use a range of sources to find out more.
		Question	I can ask further questions to deepen my understanding.
	Problem-solve	Plan	I can plan a more complex task, setting targets for completion, with some support.
		Make choices	I can sort information and choose what is relevant.
		Reason	I can break down complex ideas in to steps to reason.
	Apply knowledge	Form opinions	I can give an opinion about someone else's work.
		Apply knowledge	I can look for relationships between things and draw conclusions.
Reflective learners	Evaluation	Reflect	I can draw out lessons and generalisations from my reflections and discuss them.
		Revise	I can monitor how things are going and make revisions.
Creative thinkers	Creativity	Use imagination	I can use my imagination to see things in my 'mind's eye'.
		Lateral thinking	I can give alternative solutions or explanations.
		Meta-learning	I can describe effective learning and compare it to my own.
Self-managers	Motivation	Persevere	I recognise when I need to try a different approach and I keep trying.
		Manage distractions	I know how to manage classroom distractions.
		Set goals	I can break a longer term plan into achievable steps.
	Emotional skills	Be self-aware	I can talk about my strengths and weaknesses.
		Manage my feelings	I stay calm when I find things difficult.
		Understand others' feelings	I can 'hot seat' a character or answer questions in role.

EVALUATION AND ASSESSMENT IN PRIMARY ART

Team workers	Social skills	Be independent	I use strategies I have been taught to help myself when I'm stuck.
		Collaborate, value & support others	I can work with others to deepen my learning.
		Communicate	I can explain ideas and processes.
		Listen	I can listen and respond in formal and informal situations.
YEAR 5		KEY SKILL	'I' STATEMENT
Independent enquirers	Enquire	Be curious	I am curious about things and persevere to find answers to complex questions.
		Question	I can construct hypothetical questions.
	Problem-solve	Plan	I can plan a longer activity, breaking it into manageable steps and setting targets for completion with minimal adult support.
		Make choices	I can choose how to present information.
		Reason	I can use inference and deduction to offer explanations.
	Apply knowledge	Form opinions	I can make a constructive judgement about someone else's work.
		Apply knowledge	I can apply my learning to review situations.
Reflective learners	Evaluation	Reflect	I can use a range of criteria to reflect on my own and others' learning.
		Revise	I can use insight to revise my work.
Creative thinkers	Creativity	Use imagination	I can use my imagination to see things in my 'mind's eye'.
		Lateral thinking	I can look for alternative innovative outcomes.
		Meta-learning	I understand how I learn best.
Self-managers	Motivation	Persevere	I understand that learning occurs when we make mistakes and learn from them.
		Manage distractions	I know what conditions are best for my learning.
		Set goals	I can set success criteria in a group and reflect on achievements.
	Emotional skills	Be self-aware	I understand how my self-image can affect my learning.
		Manage my feelings	I can use positive self-talk.
		Understand others' feelings	I can appreciate a range of feeling and viewpoints, even when they differ from my own.

EVALUATION AND ASSESSMENT IN PRIMARY ART

Team workers	Social skills	Be independent	I can work independently.
		Collaborate, value & support others	I can motivate all members of the group to contribute and remind them of the task.
		Communicate	I understand differences of opinion and respond positively.
		Listen	I can use body language to enhance my listening.
YEAR 6		KEY SKILL	'I' STATEMENT
Independent enquirers	Enquire	Be curious	I can explore things which don't interest me much.
		Question	I understand that questions can have more than one correct answer and some cannot be answered.
	Problem-solve	Plan	I can independently plan a complex task, anticipating blocks and applying a range of skills.
		Make choices	I can choose what is relevant and present information in an appropriate format.
		Reason	I can debate using a reasoned, logical argument.
	Apply knowledge	Form opinions	I can listen to a range of opinions and make my own decisions.
		Apply knowledge	I can make a mind map to show links in my thinking and learning.
Reflective learners	Evaluation	Reflect	I can develop my own criteria and reflect on my own and others' learning.
		Revise	I can make revisions based on the advice of others.
Creative thinkers	Creativity	Use imagination	I can use my imagination to rehearse things mentally.
		Lateral thinking	I can adapt and apply my learning to new situations.
		Meta-learning	I can choose to work in a way which suits my learning style.
Self-managers	Motivation	Persevere	I can use a range of strategies to become 'unstuck' & carry on.
		Manage distractions	I am a role model for good learning behaviour.
		Set goals	I can break a long-term plan into small achievable steps, plan to overcome obstacles, set success criteria and celebrate achievement.
	Emotional skills	Be self-aware	I know my feelings change over time and that I have the capacity to cope with this.
		Manage my feelings	I can acknowledge my feelings and use a range of strategies to support myself.
		Understand others' feelings	I can empathise with others, being aware that people express emotions in different ways.

EVALUATION AND ASSESSMENT IN PRIMARY ART

Team workers	Social skills	Be independent	I can identify my own learning needs.
		Collaborate, value & support others	I can use the strengths of others I work with.
		Communicate	I can adjust the way I talk to a range of situations.
		Listen	I can read the body language of others to enhance my listening.

CHAPTER SUMMARY

In this chapter, we have talked through a range of considerations about evaluation and assessment in primary art. Some key messages are that assessment should take place to recognise the importance of children's knowledge, understanding and skill progression; formative assessment – particularly questioning – offers a good way of building children's awareness and confidence. Key habits of mind are important criteria to inform assessment of children's learning, as creative thinkers, and especially in art.

REFERENCES AND FURTHER READING

Clark, I. (2015) Formative Assessment: Translating High-Level Curriculum Principles into Classroom Practice. *The Curriculum Journal*, 26 (1), 91–114.

Eisner, E. (2002) *The Arts and the Creation of Mind*. New Haven, CT: Yale University Press.

Ofsted (2009) Drawing Together: Art, Craft and Design in Schools 2005–2008. Available online: http://dera.ioe.ac.uk/10624/1/Drawing%20together.pdf

Ofsted (2012) Making a Mark: Art, Craft and Design Education. Available online: https://www.gov.uk/government/uploads/system/uploads/attachment_data/file/413330/Making_a_mark_-_art_craft_and_design_education_2008-11.pdf

Swaffield, S. (2009) *The Misrepresentation of Assessment for Learning – and the Woeful Waste of a Wonderful Opportunity*. https://impact.chartered.college/article/budden-student-learning-independence-assessment-learning/

SUGGESTED WEBSITES

SEAD assessment information: http://www.nsead.org/curriculum-resources/assessment_and_progression.aspx

CHAPTER 9

CONCLUSIONS

Figure 9.1 Three ways special school, Bath

This book has invited a renewed look at teaching art creatively, addressing important implications for learning and pedagogy. It highlights the adult's role as co-participative and inclusive, where discourse and the co-construction of knowledge are both vital. Central to this is a democratic notion of creativity: adults and children working together to seek new connections in a climate of creative enquiry.

A willingness to observe, listen and work closely with children's ideas has developed in a community of adults who understand what it means to be creative, who are interested in how children learn and who model the creative process alongside children. Providing vital, rich and creative learning opportunities, with openness to possibility, has generated depth in collaborative learning.

Creativity embraces the way in which children can develop new ideas, helping them build unique conceptual frameworks. We build creative frameworks through

■ ■ ■ ■ CONCLUSIONS

the interaction with the ideas of other learners and creative experts. Creativity requires a curriculum that gives space, time and attention to creative learning and creative teaching.

A systematic review of recent literature by Davies *et al.* (2013) concluded that three key aspects of school culture are vital in nurturing children's creativity: the physical environment, the pedagogical environment, and partnerships beyond schools. Key features of the pedagogical environment included adults who modelled creativity and valued purposeful risk-taking as co-participants in work of personal significance and time and space for experimentation and uncertainty.

THE CHILD AT THE HEART OF THE PROCESS

Children will always come up with good ideas and have unexpected theories that are purposeful and imaginative. Careful observations of children provide an insight into their interests and preoccupations. The adults facilitate and support the children's depth of learning by respecting their individual interests and taking time to make connections with the children's thinking. The emphasis is on supporting children's developing ideas, thoughts and feelings. Children have opportunities for exploration, and for response and contextualisation of their learning, using innovative and imaginative approaches that stimulate the imagination and encourage independent thought.

If adults take children's ideas seriously, they can support children in the exploration and expression of their ideas in a hundred languages. Documentation to 'make the learning visible' is an integral tool for both the expression of ideas and meaning making.

THE SIGNIFICANCE OF THE ARTS

The arts have the power to be transformational in our lives; they are important because they are essential in understanding what it is to be human. The arts enrich our daily experience and give us a sense of personal, social and cultural identity. The arts open up new possibilities and the notion of learning as a multi-dimensional concept. The arts allow the exploration of big themes: identity, belonging, community, relationships, conflict, birth and death. Giving attention to different interpretations and fluid meanings in constructing knowledge has generated 'possibility thinking with wisdom' (Craft 2005).

Working alongside creative professional artists is a privilege that all children and adults should have access to: to be able to learn together in ways which value our human capacities for being creative, for being artists.

THE POWER OF CHILDREN'S IMAGINATION

World expert on creativity Sir Ken Robinson said that 'our imagination is the unique human capacity to bring into our minds things that aren't present and to be able to hypothesise about what might be'.

Children are born equipped with amazing imaginative and creative capacities. These include the powerful drive to explore, hypothesise, make connections and communicate ideas. Playfulness and exploration are at the heart of children's ways of

CONCLUSIONS

working out their place in the world. Remember your own childhood and how your own imagination allowed you to free-flow with ideas – seeing faces in tree trunks, building stories in the sand, making magic potions. Children's imagination is an essential element of their own creativity. Children need time, space and the freedom to be creative, to take inspiration from the world around them and from inside their creative minds. Children wonder, reflect on their experiences and can communicate their thoughts and feelings in 100 languages.

Everyone is born with creative potential to learn through play and our imagination. We can all see images in the clouds – we can imagine the most unusual things. Our imagination frees our mind to think differently, to play with possibilities. We daydream and mind-wander – these processes are not to be undervalued. Some of the best ideas happen in unexpected ways, often combining experience with imagination.

As teachers, we need to think about how best to nurture the power of children's imagination and creativity as a habit of mind and how we make a place for this in our everyday lives. Children's imagination is powerful – it is everywhere. Children inhabit their imagination. Children have an innate capacity to be curious. Children are explorers and creative knowledge builders. They don't stop imagining, thinking, feeling or learning through all their senses – inside and outside school, at home, in the light and in the dark.

Imagination invites potential and possibility – 'where we might be able to go and what we might be able to do' in every present situation, exploring the liminal space between ideas and materials to make meaning. As adults, we can invite children to have the freedom to follow their fascinations, to play in environments of enquiry, to imagine, to wonder. This is what the late Anna Craft called 'possibility thinking' – to ask the questions 'What If?' and 'What as if?'

We are all guardians of children's creativity and imagination. I think we should challenge current orthodoxies in our performance-led education system and work towards system change. High standards and creativity do not need to be polarised. We shouldn't prioritise a deficit or transmission model of learning that is prescriptive and closes down children's ideas. In fact, children ask great questions: How can we bring the outside inside? How big does a map have to be to be in it? Children are great at showing how the imagination is powerful. When children are in the flow, they are immersed in possibility. Imagination is infinite.

The arts particularly allow us to explore different versions of ourselves, inviting children to engage in open-ended activities and multi-modal learning – expressing their ideas in 100 languages of learning and through all their senses. Children move easily between modalities; they play, sing, act, draw, paint and make. Imagine a world where our children are engaged in serious creative play, where their environments are full of space and light, where adults – creative adults who show a deep respect for children's ideas, theories and fascinations – are companions in the children's enquiries about the world.

In Bath, our creative education project 'School Without Walls' is living this out daily – it creates spaces to dream, think, explore and experiment – breaking down the barriers between cultural centres and schools. But it requires courage and purposeful risk taking – it is a creative disruption. 'School Without Walls' is doing school differently. The city is a campus for learning. Children are agents of their own learning, as active citizens, co-designing learning alongside adults who trust in

CONCLUSIONS

children's ideas, their imagination, curiosity and questions – giving them time, space and quality attention.

Another example of this everyday activism is the 'House of Imagination', which was launched by Sir Ken Robinson at the Creative Revolution conference at Bath Spa University and which invites children and young people to explore ideas in a studio environment alongside creative professionals – mathematicians, philosophers, scientists, artists and architects – to empower children to explore their imagination and express their ideas. Processes of enquiry, not necessarily products, are valued. Failure is fine; in fact, it's essential! Watch a child at play. To them all things are possible. Their eyes light up with learning. This wide-eyed view on the world is liberating. Finlay, 9, recently described their imagination as 'a fizzing mass of energy'.

The arts have the power to be transformational in all of our lives. 'Forest of Imagination', inspired by Grant Associates' Gardens by the Bay (itself an example of human creative genius), is a pop-up contemporary arts and architecture and creative learning event in Bath that reimagines public spaces in the city and invites everyone to explore their own imagination and creativity, highlighting the power of nature to inspire.

To quote Andrew Grant: 'Forest is the home of Imagination. Imagination is everyone'.

Children's imaginations can run wild. Adults are also inspired by the power of children's imaginations – with ingenious and thought-provoking ideas full of joy.

We want to create spaces that inspire and feed the creativity of our children. Forest of Imagination deliberately brings the inspirational experience and sensations of nature and wildness to our doorsteps – it is about the creative ecology of the city, with collaboration across generations and between industries. Creative installations in the heart of the city and in nature address bigger themes about the environment and climate change, sharing ideas through our collective imagination.

I am profoundly convinced that children's love of learning can be nurtured through providing stimulating, engaging and creative experiences that will develop life-long and life-wide creative habits for life. Children are 'enemies of boredom' – they explore their imagination through play, through discovery and making, in landscapes of possibility and environments of encounter.

However, the future is uncertain. We live in a world that is changing rapidly, and we need creative thinkers to make a difference to our society. Imagining possibilities and exploring ideas are vital to creative solutions. What we need is a creative and imaginative way of being in the world alongside children, to respect their ideas and their ingenuity in coming up with solutions, and to think differently – alongside adults who care.

The World Economic Forum has proposed that the three main capacities required for future society are creative and critical thinking and complex problem-solving. The arts particularly teach children that problems can have more than one creative solution, that questions can be interpreted in many ways and have more than one answer, and that there are many ways to see and interpret the world in subtle and extraordinary ways.

Children are now – we are not just preparing them for the future. Every child has a right to the arts, creativity and culture no matter what their background or circumstance. As adults, we need to support children's creative thinking and feeling and to

CONCLUSIONS

allow children's ideas to collide and connect, to problem-solve, and to understand what it is to be human. We need to create a culture for imagination and creativity to flourish, for children to develop a love learning, and for learning to be irresistible.

This active idea of imagination opens up the world to better ways of thinking and working together. It helps us to learn to move, like artists, from open possibility to accomplishment and actualisation. It offers a sense of shared, beneficial possibility – and beauty – that becomes powerful when it is nurtured within our communities as creativity for good. It is children who will light up the future and imagine new possibilities, full of hope and wonder.

I am proposing the need for a grassroots revolution to embed creativity in children's learning and to develop creative schools. One of my long-term ambitions is the changing of mindsets in schools so that art education can help to develop children's self-directed and self-determined enquiry. This invites the creation of a new culture of schooling that has as much to do with the cultivation of dispositions as with the acquisition of skills. Teaching art creatively is at the centre of this paradigm shift.

10 principles in conclusion

1. Everyone is born with creative potential.
2. Environments of enquiry: structure and freedom
3. Freedom to follow fascinations and explore ideas in 100 languages
4. Children as agents in their own learning, as active citizens
5. Trust in children's and young people's ideas, their curiosity and questions – imagining possibilities
6. Processes of enquiry, not necessarily products
7. Failure is fine; in fact, it's essential!
8. Dialogue, relationships and companionship – time, space and attention
9. Life-wide and life-long creative capacities are essential life skills.
10. Creative and critical thinking and complex problem solving

Figure 9.2 Kinder Garden, Bath

ACKNOWLEDGEMENT

With huge thanks to all the children, teachers and artists we have worked with over many years.

REFERENCES AND FURTHER READING

Alexander, R. (Ed.) (2010) *Children, Their World, Their Education: Final Report and Recommendations of the* Cambridge Primary Review. London: Routledge.

Craft, A. (2005) *Creativity in Schools: Tensions and Dilemmas*. London: Routledge.

Craft, A., Cremin, T., and Burnard, P. (Eds.) (2008) *Creative Learning 3-11 and How We Document It*. Stoke-on-Trent, UK: Trentham Publisher.

Davies, D., Jindal-Snape, D., Collier, C., Digby, R., Hay, P., and Howe, A. (2013) Creative Learning Environments in Education—A Systematic Literature Review. *Thinking Skills and Creativity*, 8, 80–91.

Jones, R. and Wyse, D. (Eds.) (2013) *Creativity in the Primary Curriculum*. London: David Fulton.

National Advisory Committee on Creative and Cultural Education (1999) *All Our Futures: Creativity, Culture and Education*. Sudbury, UK: Department for Education and Employment.

Rose, J. (2009) *Primary Curriculum Review*. London: Department for Children Schools and Families.

APPENDIX
RESOURCES AND PUBLICATIONS

WHICH ARTIST?

The following list of artists can be used to inform children's understanding of artists' work. It is intended as a key teaching resource for supporting work both in art and design and across the curriculum. It can be used as a first point of reference in identifying artists related to specific themes and genres.

What follows is not a prescriptive list or by any means definitive: instead, it aims to help teachers to provide a context for looking at artists' work. We have included examples by men and women, both historical and contemporary and work made in different contexts, styles and cultures.

There are over 80 themes arranged alphabetically which feature five prominent examples, including dates. These include both art-specific and topic-based themes as well as principal art movements.

Many of the images are available as posters/reproductions from **Shorewood Educational**, the leading educational publisher providing an extensive range of reproductions of the work of artists, craftspeople and designers from around the world.

ABSTRACT ART

Ayres, Gillian (1930–)
Hodgkin, Howard (1932–2017)
Kandinsky, Wassily (1866–1944)
Pollock, Jackson (1912–1956)
Rothko, Mark (1903–1970)

ABSTRACT EXPRESSIONISM

De Kooning, Willem (1904–1997)
Kline, Franz (1910–1962)
Newman, Barnett (1905–1970)

Pollock, Jackson (1912–1956)
Rothko, Mark (1903–1970)

ADVERTISING & MEDIA

Davis, Stuart (1894–1964)
Hamilton, Richard (1922–2011)
Lichtenstein, Roy (1923–1997)
Toulouse-Lautrec, Henri (1864–1901)
Warhol, Andy (1928–1987)

ARCHITECTURE

Christo, Javacheff (1935–2020)
Gaudi, Antonio (1852–1926)
Hadid Zaha (1950–2016)
Leger, Fernand (1881–1955)
Rogers, Richard (1933–)

ART DECO

Cliff, Clarice (1899–1972)
Laurencin, Marie (1885–1956)
Lempicka, Tamara de (1898–1980)
Philpott, Glynn (1884–1937)
Rivera, Diego (1886–1957)

ART NOUVEAU

Beardsley, Aubrey (1872–1898)
Gaudi, Antonin (1852–1926)
Mackintosh, Charles Rennie (1868–1928)
Mucha, Alphonse (1860–1939)
Tiffany glass (19th and 20th Century)

ASSEMBLAGE

Beuys, Joseph (1921–1986)
Broodthaers, Marcel (1924–1976)
Cornell, Joseph (1903–1972)
Messager, Annette (1943–)
Rauschenberg, Robert (1925–2008)

BAUHAUS

Albers, Josef (1888–1976)
Gropius, Walter (1883–1969)

APPENDIX

　　Kandinsky, Wassily (1866–1944)
　　Klee, Paul (1879–1940)
　　Moholy-Nagy, László (1895–1946)

BAROQUE

　　Caravaggio (1571–1610)
　　Rubens, Peter Paul (1577–1640)
　　Sánchez Cotán, Juan (1561–1637)
　　Velázquez, Diego (1599–1660)
　　Zurbarán, Franciscode (1598–1664)

BIRDS & ANIMALS

　　Flannigan, Barry (1941–2009)
　　Frink, Elizabeth (1930–1993)
　　Landseer, Edward (1802–1873)
　　Rousseau, Henri (1844–1910)
　　Stubbs, George (1724–1806)

BODY

　　Bourgeois, Louise (1911–2010)
　　Da Vinci, Leonardo (1452–1519)
　　Freud, Lucien (1922–2011)
　　Gericault, Theodore (1791–1824)
　　Spencer, Stanley (1891–1959)

BRITAIN SINCE 1930

　　Lowry, Lawrence Stephen (1887–1973)
　　Moore, Henry (1898–1986)
　　Nash, Paul (1889–1946)
　　Nicholson, Ben (1894–1982)
　　Weight, Carel (1908–1997)

BUILT ENVIRONMENT

　　Gropius, Walter (1883–1969)
　　Le Corbusier (1887–1965)
　　Lowry, Lawrence (1887–1973)
　　Malevich, Kazimir (1878–1935)
　　Paolozzi, Eduardo (1924–2005)

CARNIVAL

　　Degas, Edgar (1834–1917)
　　Gertler, Mark (1891–1939)

Hockney, David (1937–)
Johnson, William H. (1901–1970)
Picasso, Pablo (1881–1973)

CITYSCAPES

Caillebotte, Gustave (1848–1894)
Canaletto (Antonio Canale) (1697–1768)
Hopper, Edward (1882–1967)
Lowry, Lawrence (1887–1973)
Utrillo, Maurice (1883–1955)

CLOTHES & COSTUME

Blake, Peter (1932–)
Clouet, Francois (1522–1572)
Hilliard, Nicholas (1547–1619)
Japanese prints (17th to 19th Century)
Shonibare Yinka (1962–)

COLLAGE

Ernst, Max (1891–1976)
Gris, Juan (1887–1927)
Matisse, Henri (1869–1954)
Picasso, Pablo (1881–1973)
Schwitters, Kurt (1887–1948)

COLOUR

Delaunay, Sonia (1885–1979)
Frankenthaler, Helen (1928–2011)
Hodgkin, Howard (1932–2017)
Matisse, Henri (1869–1954)
Rothko Mark (1903–1970)

CONCEPTUAL ART

Beuys, Joseph (1921–1986)
Duchamp, Marcel (1887–1968)
Long, Richard (1945–)
Nauman, Bruce (1941–)
Oppenheim, M. (1913–1985)

CONSTRUCTIVISM

Gabo, Naum (1890–1977)
Lissitzky, Eleazer (1890–1941)

APPENDIX

Moholy-Nagy, László (1895–1946)
Rodchenko, Alexander (1891–1956)
Tatlin, Vladimir (1885–1953)

CUBISM

Braque, George (1882–1963)
Feininger, Lyonel (1871–1956)
Gris, Juan (1887–1927)
Leger, Fernand (1881–1955)
Picasso, Pablo (1881–1973)

DADA

Duchamp, Marcel (1887–1968)
Grosz, George (1893–1959)
Hoch, Hannah (1889–1978)
Man Ray (1890–1976)
Schwitters, Kurt (1887–1948)

DRAWING

Durer, Albert (1471–1528)
Giacometti, Alberto (1901–1966)
Hockney, David (1937–)
Michelangelo Buonarroti (1475–1564)
Schiele, Egon (1890–1918)

DREAMS & THE IMAGINATION

Aboriginal dream paintings (Indigenous tradition)
Bosch, Hieronymus (1450–1516)
Chagall, Marc (1887–1985)
Dali, Salvador (1904–1989)
Magritte, Rene (1898–1967)

ENVIRONMENT

Goldsworthy, Andy (1956–)
Long, Richard (1945–)
Nash, Paul (1889–1946)
O'Keeffe, Georgia (1887–1986)
Rousseau, Henri (1844–1910)

EXPRESSIONISM

Beckmann, Max (1884–1950)
Kirchner, Ernst (1880–1938)

Kandinsky, Wassily (1866–1944)
Marc, Franz (1880–1916)
Nolde, Emil (1867–1956)

FAMILY

Cassatt, Mary (1844–1926)
Johnson, W H (1901–1970)
Raphael (1483–1520)
Rego, Paula (1935–)
Wood, Tom (1952–)

FANTASY

Blake, William (1757–1827)
Crane, Walter (1845–1913)
Klee, Paul (1879–1940)
Rackham, Arthur (1867–1939)
Redon, Odilon (1840–1916)

FARMING

Breughel, Pieter (1525–1569)
Millet, Jean-Francois (1814–1875)
Miro, Joan (1893–1983)
Rothenstein, Michael (1908–1993)
Wood, Grant (1892–1942)

FORM

Hesse, Eva (1936–1970)
Hepworth, Barbara (1904–1975)
Kapoor, Anish (1954–)
Mach David (1956–)
Whiteread, Rachel (1963–)

FAUVISM

Derain, Andre (1880–1954)
Dufy, Raoul (1877–1953)
Matisse, Henri (1869–1954)
Van Dongen, Kees (1877–1968)
Vlaminck, Maurice de (1876–1954)

FILM & VIDEO

Horn, Rebecca (1944–)
Klein, Yves (1928–1962)

APPENDIX

Paik, Nam June (1932–)
Park, Nick (1958–)
Viola, Bill (1951–)

FLOWERS & GARDENS

Klimt, Gustav (1862–1918)
Nolde, Emil (1867–1956)
O'Keeffe, Georgia (1887–1986)
Redon, Odilon (1840–1916)
Rivera, Diego (1886–1957)

FOOD & DRINK

Archimboldo, Giuseppe (1527–1593)
Oldenburg, Claus (1929–)
Renoir, Auguste (1841–1919)
Sánchez Cotán, Juan (1561–1637)
Warhol, Andy (1928–1987)

FORCES & MOVEMENT

Balla, Giacomo (1871–1958)
Bomberg, David (1890–1957)
Marc, Franz (1880–1916)
Severini, Gino (1883–1966)
Vasarely, Victor (1908–1997)

FORM

Cragg, Tony (1949–)
Frink, Elizabeth (1930–1993)
Kapoor, Anish (1954–)
Moore, Henry (1898–1986)
Whiteread, Rachel (1963–)

FUTURISM

Balla, Giacomo (1871–1958)
Boccioni, Umberto (1882–1916)
Carra, Carlo (1881–1966)
Severini, Gino (1883–1966)

IDENTITY

Blake, Peter (1932–)
Boyce, Sonia (1962–)

Gilbert and George (1942/3–)
Kahlo, Frida (1907–1954)
Shonibare, Yinka (1963–)

ILLUSTRATION

Blake, Quentin (1932–)
Blake, William (1757–1827)
Foreman, Michael (1938–)
Ray, Jane (1959–)
Scalfe, Gerald (1936–)

IMPRESSIONISM

Manet, Edouard (1832–1883)
Monet, Claude (1840–1926)
Morisot, Berthe (1841–1895)
Renoir, Pierre Auguste (1841–1919)
Sisley, Alfred (1839–1899)

INSTALLATION

Hamilton, Richard (1922–2011)
Horn, Rebecca (1944–)
Keinholtz, Edward (1927–1994)
Viola, Bill (1951–)
Wentworth, Richard (1947–)

INTERIORS

Bonnard, Pierre (1867–1947)
De Hooch, Pieter (1629–1684)
Hamilton, Richard (1922–2011)
Matisse, Henri (1869–1954)
Vermeer, Jan (1632–1675)

INTERNATIONAL GOTHIC

Cimambue (active: 1272–1302)
Duccio (1255–1319)
Limbourg Brothers (active: 1400–1416)
Lorenzetti, Ambrogio (active: 1319–1348)
Martini, Simone (1284–1344)

KINETIC ART

Calder, Alexander (1898–1975)
Horn, Rebecca (1944–)

APPENDIX

Riley, Bridget (1931–)
Tinguely, Jean (1928–1991)
Vasaraly, Victor (1908–1997)

LANDSCAPES

Breughel, Pieter the Elder (1525–1569)
Cezanne, Paul (1839–1906)
Constable, John (1776–1837)
Lorraine, Claude (1600–1682)
Sutherland, Graham (1903–1980)

LIGHT

Caravaggio (1571–1610)
Holzer, Jenny (1950–)
Monet, Claude (1840–1926)
Riley, Bridget (1931–)
Seurat, Georges (1859–1891)

LINE

Calder, Alexander (1898–1975)
Klee, Paul (1879–1940)
Mondrian, Piet (1872–1944)
Riley, Bridget (1931–)
Twombly, Cy (1928–)

MATERIALS

Berni, Antonio (1905–1981)
Blacker, Kate (1955–)
Hartoum, Mona 1952–)
Hesse, Eva (1936–1970)
Tapies, Antoni (1923–2012)

MYTHS & LEGENDS

Botticelli, Sandro (1445–1510)
Hunt, William Holman (1827–1910)
Indian miniatures
Rego, Paula (1935–)
Spencer, Stanley (1891–1959)

OBJECTS

Cornell, Joseph (1903–1972)
Cragg, Tony (1949–)

APPENDIX

de Vaal Edmund (1959–)
Duchamp, Marcel (1887–1968)
Man Ray (1890–1976)

OURSELVES

Blake, Peter (1932–)
Boyce, Sonia (1962–)
Modigliani, Amadeo (1884–1920)
Munch, Edvard (1863–1944)
Sherman, Cindy (1954–)

PAINTING

De Kooning, Willem (1904–1997)
Hamling, Maggie (1945–)
Hodgkin, Howard (1932–2017)
Johns, Jasper (1930–)
Van Gogh, Vincent (1853–1890)

PATTERN

Aboriginal Art
African Art
Aztec Art
Islamic Art
Roman Mosaic

PEOPLE AT WORK

Breughel, Pieter the Elder (1525–1569)
Leger, Fernand (1881–1955)
Lowry, Lawrence (1887–1973)
Millet, Jean-Francois (1814–1875)
Segal, George (1924–2021)

PHOTOGRAPHY

Adams, Ansel (1902–1984)
Doisneau, Robert (1912–1994)
Man Ray (1890–1976)
Richter, Gerhard (1932–)
Sherman, Cindy (1954–)

POP ART

Blake, Peter (1932–)
Johns, Jasper (1930–)

APPENDIX

Lichtenstein, Roy (1923–1997)
Warhol, Andy (1928–1987)
Wesselmann, Tom (1931–)

PORTRAITS

Hilliard, Nicolas (1547–1619)
Holbein, Hans (1497–1543)
Schad, Christian (1894–1982)
Watt, Alison (1965–)
Wood, Grant (1892–1942)

POST-IMPRESSIONISM

Gauguin, Paul (1848–1903)
Pissarro, Camille (1831–1903)
Seurat, Georges (1859–1891)
Signac, Paul (1863–1935)
Van Gogh, Vincent (1853–1890)

PRE-RAPHAELITE

Brown, Ford Maddox (1821–1893)
Burne-Jones, Sir Edward (1833–1898)
Hunt, William Holman (1827–1910)
Millais, Sir John Everett (1829–1896)
Rossetti, David Gabriel (1828–1882)

PRINTMAKING

Dine, Jim (1935–)
Durer, Albrecht (1471–1528)
Ernst, Max (1891–1976)
Rauschenberg, Robert (1925–2008)
Spero, Nancy (1926–2009)

RECYCLING

Berni, Antonio (1905–1981)
Cragg Tony (1949–)
Rauschenberg, Robert (1925–)
Schnabel, Julian (1951–)
Schwitters, Kurt (1887–1948)

RENAISSANCE

Botticelli, Sandro (1445–1510)
Da Vinci, Leonardo (1452–1519)

Donatello, (1386–1466)
Michelangelo (1475–1564)
Raphael (1483–1520)

ROMANTICISM

Blake, William (1757–1827)
Church, Frederick (1826–1900)
Constable, John (1776–1837)
Goya, Francisco (1746–1828)
Turner, J.M.W. (1775–1850)

SCULPTURE

Frink, Elizabeth (1930–1993)
Giacometti, Alberto (1877–1966)
Gormley, Anthony (1950–)
Hartoum, Mona (1952–)
Rodin, August (1840–1917)

SEASCAPES

Carmichael, John (1800–1868)
Hiroshige, Ando (1797–1858)
Knight, Laura (1877–1970)
Turner, J.M.W. (1775–1850)
Wallis, Alfred (1855–1942)

SEASONS

Avercamp, Hendrick (1585–1634)
Botticelli, Sandro (1445–1510)
Gauguin, Paul (1848–1903)
Monet, Claude (1840–1926)
Palmer, Samuel (1805–1881)

SELF-PORTRAITS

Blake, Peter (1932–)
Gilbert (1943–) and George (1942–)
Kahlo, Frida (1910–1954)
Spencer, Stanley (1891–1959)
Van Gogh, Vincent (1853–1890)

SHAPE

Green, Anthony (1927–)
Kelly, Ellsworth (1923–1965)

APPENDIX

Klee, Paul (1879–1940)
Matisse, Henri (1869–1954)
Stella, Frank (1936–)

SOUND

Horn, Rebecca (1944–)
Kandinsky, Wassily (1866–1944)
Motley, Archibald (1891–1981)
Rauschenberg, Robert (1925–2008)
Tinguely, Jean (1928–1991)

SPACE

Fontana, Lucio (1899–1968)
Gabo, Naum (1890–1977)
Malevich, Kasimir (1878–1935)
Newman, Barnett (1905–1970)
Rothko, Mark (1903–1970)

SPORTS & PASTIMES

Blake, Peter (1932–)
Pieter Bruegel the Elder (1525–1569)
Homer, Winslow (1836–1910)
Inshaw, David (1943–)
Rockwell, Norman (1894–1978)

STILL LIFE

Blackadder, Elizabeth (1931–)
Cragg, Tony (1949–)
De Heem, Jan (1606–1683)
Picasso, Pablo (1881–1973)
Sanchez-Cotan, Juan (1561–1637)

STORIES

Kitaj, R.B. (1932–2007)
Rego, Paula (1935–2022)
Ringgold, Faith (1930–)
Sassetta (1932–1450)
Spencer, Stanley (1891–1959)

SYMBOLISM

Beckmann, Max (1884–1950)
Dali, Salvador (1904–1989)

Hilliard, Nicholas (1547–1619)
Kahlo, Frida (1907–1954)
Van Eyck, Jan (1422–1441)

SURREALISM

Dali, Salvador (1904–1989)
Delvaux, Paul (1897–1994)
Ernst, Max (1891–1976)
Magritte, Rene (1898–1967)
Miro, Joan (1893–1983)

TEXTURE

Brennand-Wood, Michael (1959–)
Caprara, Julia (1939–2008)
Ernst, Max (1880–1938)
Rauschenberg, Robert (1925–2008)
Stella, Frank (1936–)

TONE

Auerbach, Frank (1931–)
De la Tour, George (1593–1652)
El Greco (1541–1614)
Grimshaw, Atkinson (1836–1893)
Monet, Claude (1840–1926)

TOYS & GAMES

Blackadder, Elizabeth (1931–)
Pieter Bruegel the Elder (1525–1569)
Cornell, Joseph (1903–1972)
Koons, Jeff (1955–)
Rivera, Diego (1886–1957)

TUDORS AND STUARTS

Dyck, Anthony van (1599–1641)
Elizabethan miniatures (16th/17th century)
Hilliard, Nicholas (1547–1619)
Holbein, Hans (1497–1543)
Rubens, Peter Paul (1577–1640)

VICTORIANS

Cassatt, Mary (1845–1927)
Degas, Edgar (1843–1917)

APPENDIX

Morisot, Berthe (1841–1895)
Sickert, Walter (1860–1942)
Toulouse-Lautrec, Henri de (1864–1901)

VORTICISM

Bomberg, David (1890–1957)
Lewis, Wyndham (1882–1957)
Epstein, Jacob (1880–1959)
Nash Paul (1889–1946)
Wadsworth Edward (1889–1949)

WAR

Bacon, Francis (1909–1992)
Delacroix, Eugene (1798–1764)
Grosz, George (1893–1959)
Nash, Paul (1889–1946)
Uccello, Paolo (1397–1475)

WATER

Hiroshige, Ando (1797–1858)
Hockney, David (1937–)
Hokusai, Katsushika (1760–1849)
Monet, Claude (1840–1926)
Renoir, Auguste (1841–1919)

KEY RECOMMENDED BOOKS, JOURNALS AND RESEARCH

Further Reading

Abbs, P. (2003) *Against the Flow. Education, the Arts and Postmodern Culture*. London, New York: Routledge Falmer.

Adams, E. (2002) Power Drawing. *Journal of Art and Design Education*, 21 (3), 220–233.

Adams, E. (2006) *Drawing Insights*. London: Drawing Power, the Campaign for Drawing.

Adams, J. (2003) The Artist-Teacher Scheme As Postgraduate Professional Development In Higher Education. *International Journal of Art and Design Education*, 22 (2), 183–194.

Adams, J. (2005) Room 13 and the Contemporary Practice of Artist-Learners. *Studies in Art Education*, 471, 23–33.

Addison, N. and Burgess, L. (Eds.) (2003) *Issues in Art and Design Teaching*. London: Routledge Falmer.

Alexander, R. (Ed.) (2009) *Children, their World, their Education: Final report and recommendations of the Cambridge Primary Review*. London: Routledge.

Atkinson, D. (2002) *Art in Education: Identity and Practice*. London: Kluwer Academic Publishers.

Banaji, S., Burn, A., and Buckingham, D. (2010) *The Rhetorics of Creativity: A Review of Literature*. London: Arts Council of England.

Bancroft, S., Fawcett, M., and Hay, P. (2008) *Researching Children Researching the World*. Stoke-on-Trent, UK: Trentham.

Clark, I. (2015) Formative Assessment: Translating High-Level Curriculum Principles into Classroom Practice. *The Curriculum Journal*, 26 (1), 91–114.

Craft, A. (2000) *Creativity across the Primary Curriculum: Framing and Developing Practice*. London: Routledge.

Craft, A. (2001) Little c Creativity. In A. Craft, B. Jeffrey and M. Leibling (Eds.), *Creativity in Education*. London: Continuum.

Craft, A. (2002) *Creativity and the Early Years: A Lifewide Foundation*. London: Continuum.

Craft, A. (2003a) Creative Thinking in the Early Years of Education. *Early Years*, 23 (2), September 2003.

Craft, A. (2003b) The Limits to Creativity in Education: Dilemmas for the Educator. *British Journal of Education Studies*, 51 (2), 113–127.

Craft, A. (2005) *Creativity in Schools: Tensions and Dilemmas*. London: Routledge.

Craft, A. and Chappell, K. (2009) Fostering Possibility through Co-researching Creative Movement with 7–11 Year Olds. In S. Blenkinsop (Ed.), *The Imagination in Education*. Cambridge Scholars Publishing.

Craft, A., Chappell, K., Cremin, T., and Jeffrey, B. (2015) *Creativity, Education and Society: Writings of Anna Craft*. Stoke-on-Trent, UK: Trentham Books.

Craft, A., Chappell, K., and Twining, P. (2008a) Learners Reconceptualising Education: Widening Participation through Creative Engagement? *Innovations in Education and Teaching International*, 45 (3), 235–245.

Craft, A., Cremin, T., Burnard, P., and Chappell, K. (2007) Teacher Stance in Creative Learning: A Study of Progression. *Thinking Skills and Creativity*, 2 (1), 136–147. Creative Partnerships.

Craft, A., Cremin, T., and Burnard, P. (Eds.) (2008b) *Creative Learning and How We Document It*. Stoke-on-Trent, UK: Trentham Books.

Craft, A. Cremin, T. Hay, P., and Clack, J. (2014) Creative Primary Schools: Developing and Maintaining Pedagogy For Creativity. *Ethnography and Education*, 9 (1), 16–34.

Craft, A., McConnon, L., and Matthews, A. (2012) Creativity and Child-Initiated Play. *Journal of Thinking Skills and Creativity*, 71, 48–61.

Cremin, T. (2006) Creativity, Uncertainty and Discomfort: Teachers as Writers. *Cambridge Journal of Education*, 36 (3), 415–433.

Cremin, T. (2015) Creative Teaching and Creative Teachers. In A. Wilson (Ed.), *Creativity in Primary Education* (3rd edition, pp. 33–44). Exeter: Learning Matters.

Cremin, T. (Ed.) (2017) *Creativity and Creative Pedagogies in the Early and Primary Years*. Abingdon: Routledge.

Cremin, T., Barnes, J., and Scoffham, S. (2009) *Creative Teaching for Tomorrow: Fostering a Creative State of Mind*. Deal: Future Creative.

Cremin, T., Chappell, K., and Craft, A. (2013) Reciprocity Between Narrative, Questioning and Imagination in the Early and Primary Years: Examining the Role of Narrative in Possibility Thinking. *Thinking Skills and Creativity*, 9, 136–151.

APPENDIX

Cremin, T., Craft, A., and Burnard, P. (2006) Pedagogy and Possibility Thinking in the Early Years. *Journal of Thinking Skills and Creativity*, 1 (2), 108–119.

Cropley, A. (2001) *Creativity in Education and Learning: A Guide for Teachers and Educators*. London: Kogan Page.

Csikszentmihalyi, M. (1990) The Domains of Creativity. In M.A. Runco and R.S. Albert (Eds.), *Theories of Creativity*. London: Sage Publications.

Csikszentmihalyi, M. (1997) *Creativity, Flow and the Psychology of Discovery and Invention*. London: Rider.

Csikszentmihalyi, M. (1998) *Optimal Experience: Psychological Studies of Flow in Consciousness*. Cambridge, UK: Cambridge University Press.

Csikszentmihalyi, M. (2002) *Flow*. London: Rider.

Cultural Learning Alliance (2011) *Key Research Findings: The Case for Cultural Learning*. London: Cultural Learning Alliance.

Dahlberg, G. (2003) Pedagogy as a Loci of an Ethics of an Encounter. In M. Bloch, K. Holmlund, I. Moqvist, and T. Popkewitz (Eds.), *Governing Children, Families and Education: Restructuring the Welfare State* (pp. 261–286). New York: Palgrave McMillan.

Dahlberg, G. and Moss, P. (2005) *Ethics and Politics in Early Childhood Education*. London: Routledge.

Dahlberg, G. and Moss, P. (2006) Introduction: Our Reggio Emilia. In C. Rinaldi (Ed.), *In Dialogue with Reggio Emilia*. London: Routledge.

Dahlberg, G., Moss, P., and Pence, A. (2007) [1999] *Beyond Quality in Early Childhood Education and Care: Languages of Evaluation*. 2nd edition. London: Routledge.

Dahlberg, G., Moss, P., and Pence, A.R. (2013) Beyond Quality. In *Early Childhood Education and Care: Postmodern Perspectives*. 3rd. London: Falmer Press.

Daichendt, G. (2010) *Artist Teacher: A Philosophy for Creating and Teaching*. Bristol: Intellect.

Davies, D., Jindal-Snape, D., Hay, P., Howe, A., Collier, C., and Digby, B. (2011) *Creative Environments for Learning in Schools: A Systematic Review of Literature Undertaken by Centre for Research in Early Scientific Learning (CRESL) at Bath Spa University in Collaboration with the University of Dundee*. Unpublished. Commissioned by Learning and Teaching Scotland.

Edwards, C., Gandini, L., and Forman, G. (Eds.) (1998) *The Hundred Languages of Children: The Reggio Emilia Approach–Advanced Reflections*. 2nd edition. Greenwich, CT: Ablex Publishing.

Eisner, E. (2002) Chapter 4, What the Arts Teach and How It Shows. *The Arts and the Creation of Mind* (pp. 70–92). New Haven, CT: Yale University Press.

Eisner, E. (2003) Artistry in education. *Scandinavian Journal of Educational Research*, 47 (3), 373–384.

Elders, L. and Hay P. (Ed.) (2012) *School without Walls: A Reflective Commentary*, 5×5×5 = creativity and the egg theatre.

Eraut, M. (1994) *Developing Professional Knowledge and Competence*. London: Routledge Falmer.

Galton, M. (2008) *Creative Practitioners in Schools and Classrooms*. London: Creative Partnerships, Arts Council England.

Gandini, L., Hill, L., Cadwell, L., and Schwall, C. (Eds.) (2005) *In the Spirit of the Studio: Learning from the Atelier of Reggio Emilia*. New York: Teachers' College Press.

Gardner, H. (1980) *Artful Scribbles: The Significance of Children's Drawings*. London: Jill Norman.

Giudici, C., Rinaldi, C., and Krechevsky, M. (2001) *Making Learning Visible: Children as Individual and Group Learners*. Cambridge, MA and Reggio Emilia: Project Zero and Reggio Children.

Glaser, M. (2008) *Drawing Is Thinking*. London: Overlook Duckworth, Peter Mayer Publishers.

Grainger, T., Burnard, P., and Craft, A. (2006) Pedagogy and Possibility Thinking in the Early Years. *Thinking Skills and Creativity*, 12, 108–119.

Grainger, T., Craft, A., and Burnard, P. (2007) *Creative Learning 3-11 and How We Document It*. Stoke-on-Trent, UK: Trentham Books.

Gude, O. (2004) Postmodern Principles: In Search of a 21st Century Art Education. *Art Education*, 57 (1), 6–14.

Gude, O. (2007) Principles of Possibility: Considerations for a 21st Century Art and Culture Curriculum. *Art Education*, 60 (1), 6–17.

Hall, C., Thomson, P., and Russell, L. (2007) Teaching Like an Artist: The Pedagogic Identities and Practices of Artists in Schools. *British Journal of Sociology of Education*, 28 (5), 605–619.

Harding, A. (Ed.) (2005) *Magic Moments: Collaboration between Artists and Young People*. London: Black Dog Publishing.

Hay, P. (2011a) Artists Interventions. *ReFocus Journal*, Autumn (10).

Hay, P. (2011b) Creativity as a Democratic Right. *NSEAD Journal*, Winter (1).

Heath, S.B. (2000) Seeing Our Way Into Learning. *Cambridge Journal of Education*, 30 (1), 121–132.

Herne, S., Cox, S., and Watts, R. (2009) *Readings in Primary Art Education*. Intellect.

Jeffrey, B. (Ed.) (2006) *Creative Learning Practices: European Experiences*. London: Tufnell Press.

Jeffrey, B. and Craft, A. (2004) Teaching Creatively and Teaching for Creativity: Distinctions and Relationships. *Educational Studies*, 30 (1), 77–87.

Jeffrey, B. and Craft, A. (2006) Creative Learning and Possibility Thinking. In B. Jeffrey (Ed.), *Creative Learning Practices: European Experiences*. London: Tufnell Press.

Jones, R. and Wyse, D. (2004) *Creativity in the Primary Curriculum*. London: David Fulton.

Laevers, F. (2015) *Making care and education more effective through wellbeing and involvement: An introduction to Experiential Education*. Research Centre for Experiential Education, University of Leuven Belgium.

Matthews, J. (1992) The Genesis of Aesthetic Sensibility. In D. Thistlewood (Ed.), *Drawing, Research and Development* (pp. 26–39). London: NSEAD and Longman.

Matthews, J. (1997) The 4 Dimensional Language of Infancy: The Interpersonal Basis of Art Praxis. *Journal of Art and Design Education*, 16 (3), 285–293.

Matthews, J. (1999) *The Art of Childhood and Adolescence: The Construction of Meaning*. London: Falmer Press.

Matthews, J. (2003) *Drawing and Painting: Children and Visual Representation*. London: Paul Chapman.

MacLure, M. (2010) The Offence of Theory. *Journal of Education Policy*, 25 (2), 277–286.

APPENDIX

National Committee for Creative and Cultural Education (1999) *All Our Futures: Creativity, Culture and Education*. Sudbury, UK: Department for Education and Employment.

Ofsted (2009) Drawing together: Art, craft and design in schools 2005–2008. Available online: http://dera.ioe.ac.uk/10624/1/Drawing%20together.pdf

Ofsted (2012) Making a mark: Art, craft and design education. Available online: https://www.gov.uk/government/uploads/system/uploads/attachment_data/file/413330/Making_a_mark_-_art_craft_and_design_education_2008-11.pdf

Pringle, E. (2006) *Learning in the Gallery: Context, Process, Outcomes*. London: Arts Council England/engage.

Pringle, E. (2008) Artists' Perspectives on Art Practice and Pedagogy. In J. Sefton-Green, (Ed.), *Creative Learning*. London: Creative Partnerships. www.creative-partnerships.com

Pringle, E. and Reiss, V. (2002) *We Did Stir Things Up: The Role of Artists in Sites for Learning*. London: Arts Council of England.

Raney, K. (1998) *Visual Literacy: Issues and Debates. A Report on the Research Project 'Framing Visual and Verbal Experience'*. London: Middlesex University.

Raney, K. (2003) *Art in Question*. London: Continuum and The Arts Council of England.

Rinaldi, C. (1998) The Thought That Sustains Educational Action. *Rechild* April 1998.

Rinaldi, C. (2001) *The Courage of Utopia' in Making Learning Visible: Children as Individual and Group Learners*. C. Guidici and C. Rinaldi with M. Krechevsky (Eds.), Cambridge, MA: Reggio Children and Project Zero, Reggio Emilia and Harvard.

Rinaldi, C. (2006) *In Dialogue with Reggio: Listening, Researching and Learning*. Oxford: Routledge.

Rinaldi, C. and Moss, P. (2004) What is Reggio? *Children in Europe*, 6.

Rogoff, B. (2003) *The Cultural Nature of Human Development*. Oxford and New York: Oxford University Press.

Rosenblatt, E. and Winner, E. (1988) The Art of Children's Drawing. *Journal of Aesthetic Education*, 22, 3–15.

Swaffield, S. (2009) *The Misrepresentation of Assessment for Learning – And the Woeful Waste of a Wonderful Opportunity*. https://impact.chartered.college/article/budden-student-learning-independence-assessment-learning/

Thomson, P., Hall, C., Jones, K., and Sefton-Green, J. (2012) *The Signature Pedagogies Project: Final Report*. London: Creativity, Culture and Education. http://www.creativetallis.com/uploads/2/2/8/7/2287089/signature_pedagogies_report_final_version_11.3.12.

United Nations Convention on the Rights of the Child. Article 31 (UNESCO 2012).

Uszyńska-Jarmoc, J. (2004) The Conception of Self in Children's Narratives. *Early Child Development and Care*, 174 (1), 81–97.

Vecchi, V. (2010) *Art and Creativity in Reggio Emilia: Exploring the Role and Potential of Ateliers in Early Childhood Education*. London: Routledge.

Woods, P. and Jeffrey, B. (1996) *Teachable Moments: The Art of Creative Teaching in Primary School*. Buckingham: Open University Press.

SUGGESTED WEBSITES

http://houseofimagination.org/
http://www.forestofimagination.org.uk/

APPENDIX

http://www.schoolwithoutwalls.org.uk/
https://www.compound13.org/
http://www.room13scotland.com
https://www.gov.uk/government/publications/national-curriculum-in-england-art-and-design-programmes-of-study
https://www.gov.uk/government/publications/education-inspection-framework
https://www.gov.uk/government/organisations/ofsted
https://www.artscouncil.org.uk/letscreate
https://www.nsead.org/
https://culturallearningalliance.org.uk/
https://www.creativitycultureeducation.org/
https://www.thersa.org/discover/publications-and-articles/reports/arts-cultural-schools
https://64millionartists.com/about/
https://www.bbc.co.uk/arts/sections/get-creative
www.room-13scotland.org.uk
www.engage.org.uk
www.tate.org.uk
http://www.thebigdraw.org/the-campaign-for-drawing

INDEX

adult, role of 91–92; companion in learning 94–95; equal opportunities 98; opportunities for reflection 95; questions for focus 93–94; resources to support learning 97; teachers 92–93; working with artists 96
affordances 27
art 154–159; allowing expression 13; assessment 137–153; case studies 64–90; children's 54–63; contemporary 54–63; formal elements of 25–26; inside/outside school 6; learning environment 114–127; learning in and through 5–6; motivation for making 3; planning experiences 128–136; power of 2–3; processes 17–53; purpose of making 2; responding to works of 5; role of adult in 91–113; teaching creatively 6; teaching lessons of 15; transformative power of 13
art, teaching 1–2
Artful Thinking Palette 57
artists, working with 96
Arts Council England 14
assessment, art 137–138; creativity 144–153; diagnostic tools 140–141; evaluation process 139; formative assessment 140; questions 143–144; responding to parents 144; reviewing work together 142–143
authentic learning 75

Batheaston Primary School 66–77, 82–84
'Being an Artist' 64–66
brushes 42

carving 49
case studies: authentic learning 75; 'Being an Artist,' 64–66; co-enquiry 76; *House of Imagination* 66–75
children: art allowing expression of 13; focusing looking of 32; guarding creativity of 8; need to grow 13; value of art in lives of 55–56; working as artists 60
clay, working with 48–49
co-enquiry 76
coiling 49
collages 50–53
colour 40–47
colouring clay 49
connections, making 21
contemporary art: value of using 58; working with artists of 59
contemporary links 22
context 22
creative practice 18–19
creativity: assessing 144–153; characteristics of 6–7
cultural links 22
curriculum, planning art experiences in 128–136

democracy 11
design 34–36
diagnostic tools, assessment 140–141
digital art 52–53
direct engagement 3
discussion, questions for promoting 22–23
diversity, celebrating 20

INDEX

drawing 28–39; design 34–36; expressive drawing 32–33; focusing children's looking 32; functions of 28; illustration 34; materials for 30; narrative drawing 33–34; observational drawing 31; paper 31; reasons for 28–30; resourcing drawing 31; sketchbooks 36–39; viewfinder 31–32
drawing, importance of 4–5

Emilia, Reggio 8
equal opportunities 98
experimentation 25
exploration 25
expressive drawing 32–33
expressive painting 45

5 × 5 × 5 = creativity *see House of Imagination*
Fleming, M. 129
form 26
formal elements 25–26
formative assessment 140

Gallery of Learning 76
gallery, visiting 60–63
Geneve, case study 76–77
great artists, notion 19

habits of mind 56–58, 147–153
high-quality art, immersion in 84
historical links 22
hollow forms 49
House of Imagination 9–10, 59; Arts Council England contribution 14; case study 66–77; habits of mind 56–58; key principles of 12; year 9, 84–85
'Hundred Languages of Children, The' 11

identity, exploring 73–75
illustration 34, 46
inclusion, celebrating 20
individuals together 11
InSEA (International Society for Education Through Art) Manifesto 14
Institute of International Visual Arts (Iniva) 20
intrinsic motivation 76

language, developing 23–25
leadership: developing role of 98; key areas 98; questions for 99; responsibilities 99–100

learning: visibility of 12
learning environment, art: characteristics 115; classroom as studio 114; display focus 123–124; display interpretation 122; equal opportunities 122–123; functions of display 121; gallery of learning 119–120; learning walls 120; materials 116–118; resources and materials checklist 125–127; visible learning 115–116
learning, art 5–6
learning, supporting 97
leather hard 50
lifelong creative learner, becoming 6–7
line 26
listening 11

Malaguzzi, Loris 8, 11
materials 3–4
media and process 21
motivation, art 3
museum, making 69–70

narrative drawing 33–34
narrative painting 46
National Curriculum 7
National Curriculum children 12
National Curriculum, problem with 55

observational drawing 31
observational painting 44
Office for Standards in Education, Children's Services and Skills (Ofsted) 18

paint exploration 42–44
paint systems 40–41
painting 40–47
paints 41
paper: drawing 31; painting 42
participation 11
pattern 26
personal experience 21
personal response 21
planning 130–131; activities 131–132; open framework for 134–135; Planning Matrix 133; starting points for 130
planning paintings 46–47
plastic 50
power of art 2–3
practical considerations 41
practices, art 27; drawing 28–39; painting 40–47; printmaking 50–53; sculpture 47–50

INDEX

printmaking 50–53
processes 3–4
processes, art 17; affordances 27; celebrating diversity 20; creative practice 18–19; developing language 23–25; experimentation 25; exploration 25; exploring different aspects of art 20–23; formal elements 25–26; practices 27–53; visual literacy 19
professional development 11
Project Zero 57

research 11
resources and materials checklist 125–126
resourcing drawing 31
respect 11
responses, art 5
responsive planning 128–129

School Without Walls 71–72
school, art inside/outside 6
sculpture 47–50
shape 26
sketchbooks 36–39
skills 3–4
slabbing 49
'Sounds of House' 85–90
space 26

St Andrew's Primary School 77–82
Studio Thinking Framework 57
subject matter 21
surface decoration 49

teachers: development 96; role of 92–93, 95
teaching creatively 6; children's creativity 8; defining 7–8
textiles 50–53
texture 26
tone 26

United Kingdom, measurements of learning in 13

viewfinder 31–32
visual arts education 54–55
visual journals 36–39
visual literacy 19
vocabulary: developing language 25

ways of seeing 19
ways of working 22
whole-school policy: considerations for writing 101–106; examples 108–112; key issues 101; procedures for writing 106–108
work, responding to 5